CW00328960

ABOUT THE AUTHOR

Paul Marsh FCIPD is a director with a City based recruitment consultancy. He has worked in the HR sector for ten years and for the 'other side' in operations previous to that. A regular contributor to various journals and magazines, this is his first business book.

HR & Other Swear Words!

Practical & Credible HRM for Beginners

Paul Marsh

HR & Other Swear Words!

Practical & Credible HRM for Beginners

Austin & Macauley

A CIP catalogue record for this title is
available from the British Library.

ISBN 978 1 905609 277

www.austinmacauley.com

First Published (2009)
Austin & Macauley Publishers Ltd.
25 Canada Square
Canary Wharf
London
E14 5LB

Printed & Bound in Great Britain

Contents

PREFACE
BEFORE WE BEGIN

'So, what do you do for a living?'

When I career changed into Human Resources (HR) over ten years ago, I scanned the bookshelves of umpteen bookshops looking for a simple text that could offer some practical advice; some lessons or examples of how I should go about things in my first role. What I found instead were heavy textbooks that were big on best practice and theory but light on good old down-to-earth reality.

I didn't really want any of this. I wanted an accessible book, written in plain English and giving a good insight into the world of HRM at the 'coalface'.

So, for a start, I don't intend for this to be a weighty tome. There is no great focus here on strategy, human capital measurement or the next big thing in HR. You will not find any long-winded detail around the main HR subjects — I leave that to countless other textbooks.

Here, instead, is a brief 'toolkit' that ensures that anyone new to operational HR management can get a good head start and minimise mistakes. In other words, this book will prevent you from having to spend too much time in the land of hindsight!

It's all too easy to work in a sector for many years, often repeating the same old routines or using the same style and believing your way to be the best, most effective way. This book can therefore act as a good refresher guide for those who have been in the HR game for a while and would benefit from other perspectives.

My ultimate goal is to shift your role from being potentially reactive, administrative and of low value to something more proactive and meaningful that delivers clear results for your business.

So who is my target audience? Obviously, HR splits into a number of specialisms but my main focus here is on the generalists who are working with the operational business on a day-to-day basis. Their main relationships are with:

- line managers
- their peer group within HR
- the various 'dotted lines' that exist to other senior manager 'stakeholders'.

Obviously, HR exists in different formats within many types of organisations. This then splits further into the private, public and not-for-profit sectors. For the purposes of this text, I popularly refer to all as 'businesses' whether profit making and commercially orientated or not.

So to the title. HR is a 'swearword'?! Well, isn't it in a lot of businesses? We'll look at this in a bit more detail later but it's fair to say that, up there with traffic wardens and the taxman, HR isn't always the most loved of professions. This is a real issue in itself and will add to your challenges, as if you need any more! Unlike many professions, HR is one of those areas that seems to demand an explanation at parties or in the pub. If you're not trying to change someone's negative view of HR you are instead fumbling around trying to describe what you do in a short but meaningful paragraph.

My aim, therefore, is to help you to become a great asset to your business and to being someone who is critical to its success. The lessons that follow are from my own and others experiences; some are considered 'best practice' and some may appear a little unorthodox: All of them are about getting things right first time as much as possible to ultimately help you towards achievement and performance.

THE REALITY

WHAT YOU'RE UP AGAINST

So, you've considered your strengths, decided that you really are a 'people' person and you're thinking of going into HR. You've made a great career choice — right? Well, just hold on a minute as you're about to stumble across a couple of initial and fundamental obstacles.

Your first obstacle — HR itself

If you pick up a copy of any HR trade journal on any given week of the year, the same typical headlines will scream out at you and can go something like this:

'HR still struggling for a seat at the board table'

'An increase in HR outsourcing feared as the profession fails to add value'

The HR trade press routinely bemoan HR's lack of credibility, lack of a seat at the table, lack of influence etc. Now, this isn't just one more overblown media focus on bad news. It's actually the reality for a lot of HR people in a lot of businesses.

Any letters page from any of these same journals will be full of comments from HR Directors, Officers, Advisors, Consultants and all will often highlight the same depressing and frustrating messages.

By the way; it's getting worse! In an effort to define to others what we are here for (and in some ways to serve as a reminder to ourselves) we now see the growth of the *HR BUSINESS PARTNER* role in recent years.

Where else do we see this in companies:

Marketing Business Partner?

Advertising Business Partner?

Finance Business Partner?

...I don't think so!!

It's yet another example of HR failing to make enough of an impact on businesses and so having to re-describe the role through job titles to help it progress!

Your second obstacle – The business itself

'It's just people stuff isn't it — anyone can do that?'

'What does HR actually do?'

'Bloody HR! — they had to stick their nose in and come up with a process didn't they?'

'Can we do this without involving HR please?!'

'Is it just about welfare and looking after the staff?'

'How do they make us money?'

Typical quotes from typical managers in typical businesses up and down the country. You see, HR just isn't TANGIBLE for many line managers and employees. It wasn't around years ago so why is it here now? What's the point of it? Well, the answer to that often can't be found simply by asking those doing the job.

Read an article with an HR Director quoted in it and invariably they will describe their mission as being to 'add value and engage the workforce to ultimately become employers of choice'.

Eh?! What's that in English? People in HR can sometimes get lost in rhetoric and laudable intentions and forget that a lot of the role is about dealing with the basics, the 'hygiene factors' around what people want to motivate them towards achieving a good standard of performance and self satisfaction.

The Irony

Years ago, HR Managers were called 'Staff Managers' and were primarily administration and welfare based. In the 80s and 90s it was 'Personnel', broadly centered around similar areas but in a beefed up way and with a stronger focus on strategy and having a clearer agenda. Now, it is 'HR' — even the words 'Human Resources' are awful and have managed to worsen people's perceptions of what it is and why it is there. But here's the thing: as time has gone on, so businesses have been increasingly faced with:

- increased competition and ever changing market conditions
- skill shortages/reduced ability to attract good people – the so called 'War for Talent'
- the challenge around retaining good people
- the growth of employment law and its associated burdens.

These are all ripe areas for HR to make a great impact with, you would think. Surely, you would consider that at no better time than now can you stand to really make a difference in HR with the right approach and skill set.

Sadly, in a lot of businesses, HR has taken these challenges and just made things complicated! Long winded resourcing strategies and the associated red tape, for example, have got in the way of what simply should have been a tactical plan around 'how we can find good people'. The challenges businesses face often become a wasted opportunity in HR as managers and employees 'switch off' from remote plans drawn up in HR, by HR and sometimes not even in consultation with the line.

Appraisals, as another example, have become another good intention that has invariably ended up as a dry, bureaucratic and compliance driven process (more on that later).

One of the often quoted phrases from HR people themselves is the objective to 'make yourself redundant' as an HR professional.

This is a kind of self-sacrificing way of becoming so good at upskilling others that you then aren't needed anymore! But what other business function would aim to devalue itself so much that it is out of a job? It is worthy to work towards passing skill and knowledge on to managers and employees so that you are less needed in the future or can be freed up for other tasks. However, this must assume that either:

– there isn't really that much for others to learn

or

– there is a great deal to learn but that's ok because everyone around you who needs the skill and knowledge is more than capable of taking it on board, is genuinely interested and wants to!

In reality, you can only pass on your role to the business and 'put yourself out of a job' if your activities are or perceived to be at a sufficiently low enough skill level to enable that to happen. For example, could every manager ever be considered as an employment law expert in the business? Would they even want to be? Do they even like the subject? The skill and knowledge level involved here is also relatively high and too great a focus on it at line manager level could even distract them from what is required in the rest of their role.

'Make yourself redundant' talk only serves to further the negative stereotype of HR as being not particularly of value and something that everyone can master.

Three key pillars

So why does HR generally have such a bad name and is considered to be of low worth, derided in 'Dilbert' and seen as a bureaucratic overhead?

It can probably be summarised in three areas:

1) A lack of credibility

2) A lack of real expertise

3) A lack of hard, tangible results

Of course, there are other variables that point to success in HR but I'm going to focus mainly on these three things only.

It is these three points that I believe will give you the greatest impact in your business and on the people within it.

LESSON 1
MASTER THE THREE PILLARS

Credibility

'The quality of being trusted and believed in, capable of persuading people that something will happen or be successful'

(Oxford Dictionary)

This is a pivotal quality that good HR people need to possess soon into their role. Why?

1) Much of the activity within HR roles is concerned with persuading, influencing, gaining trust and downright all out selling to people at all levels within the business.

2) Having credibility helps get things done. You can find solutions to business issues quicker if you are perceived as credible because people are more likely to willingly work with you.

3) HR is often one of the few functions in a business that is truly 'in the know'. HR people also have to wear multiple hats and these two things can therefore make it potentially difficult to trust you. For example, in times of need you are the welfare manager to get people back on track. You are developing managers and helping employees fulfill their aspirations. You may also, however, be protecting the business from those same people; minimising the risk of legal claims and ensuring that difficult employees cannot hurt the business and/or other people within it. No other function in the business has such contradictory objectives. Having credibility can help overcome these issues – it's vitally important in the HR field as it serves to break down wall after wall of stereotypes about the profession and the trust people will or won't have in it.

Expertise

'Having expert skill or knowledge in a particular area'

(Oxford Dictionary)

One of the other key things that can hold HR back as a profession is everyone else's perception that they could do it just as well. It's just dealing with people isn't it? — and surely everyone interacts and deals with each other in a straightforward way on a daily basis?

No, because people are complicated. You can't just press a button and hope that things fall into place neatly or know that having a particular conversation with one person will lead to them acting in the way you want them to. What motivates one person won't necessarily motivate another. We're all different, people are unpredictable and that's why HR expertise is sometimes required to know 'which buttons to press', the legal context around something, how to approach a situation or the best way to deliver a solution.

It's often just as difficult for HR people themselves to communicate with and get things done through others! We can't pull rank, we aren't normally the boss and no one actually really needs to do what HR says. You see, HR stuff just doesn't always feel like real expertise to some managers and employees and so they will sometimes do their own thing, which may also lead to negative consequences.

One of the things that doesn't help this is that many managers shouldn't be managing at all but may have taken on the job for more money or status and because 'it's only people stuff at the end of the day — it's easy'.

'So, how can I get a better salary increase this year?'
'Well, there is a management role in the London sales team if you're interested?'

The missing bit here is that they haven't realised that a different set of skills is required when it comes to people management.

Poor managers may treat their staff as they would their family and friends but the manager/subordinate relationship is far more complicated. Contracts, salaries, livelihoods, relationships and careers are all at stake.

There are different dynamics and risks associated with working relationships as opposed to a manager's domestic ones and so a different set of skills needs to come into play. When managers struggle they should be able to look to you, amongst others, to help them develop their skill.

So why choose you?

Well, not just because you're 'HR' but because they know that you have the expertise to help develop their leadership abilities, emotional intelligence or management capability. If you don't have this kind of expertise then why are you there?

People may have an idea of where their company brand should be heading but the marketing experts bring it alive.

People may have a general idea of what kind of systems they may require but the IT experts have the skilled answers.

Get it?

To illustrate in another example: Providing line management with a spreadsheet is mainly administration — anyone can probably do this to one degree or another.

What you need to do to deliver expertise is analyse, recommend, create and deliver great solutions to people issues, new opportunities etc.

This book, as I said earlier, focuses largely on the HR generalist role which generally demands you know a bit about a lot. Many individuals will also specialise but what is clear is that the expertise needed at one level or another has moved on over the years and new disciplines are always emerging:

- Management development
- Employment law
- Trade Union activity
- Reward design
- Organisational development
- Employee relations
- Learning
- Resourcing
- Corporate Social Responsibility

… and so on. Some of this list is made up of traditional fields, some are newer areas that are helping businesses become more successful.

Expertise must never be about justifying your job by creating burdensome processes and red tape and it can't be about keeping hold of information because of your own potential insecurities; you need to be able to come up with a level of expertise that people *want* and *require* from HR. Going back to the 'make yourself redundant' slogan: If your expertise is relatively low then there could indeed be a good argument for outsourcing or handing over activities to the line — lock, stock and barrel if appropriate!

But be careful. Expertise once acquired needs nurturing and developing. Once you have started in HR you can spend so much time thinking about everyone else's training, motivation etc. that often your own skill requirements are put on the back burner.

This vicious circle can result in your expertise coming only from personal experience and you run the risk of becoming less exposed to new ideas, training, thinking, theories etc.

Anyway, I'm not saying that you need to make HR all high level, mystical and drenched in difficult jargon to prove how important and necessary it is as a function. You just need to deliver a level of expertise in the same way your colleagues in Marketing, IT and Finance do that is valuable, relevant, required by the business and that ultimately gets results.

Results

So let's go back to that 'tangible' thing — more than any other support function in business, HR needs to be clear on what it delivers to the business in terms of the 'bottom line'. That's profitability for the purpose of this book.

Profitability comes from improving revenues and/or decreasing or minimising costs. HR can be instrumental in both of these key areas but two questions need addressing first:

1) What does HR actually do?

2) What are its Key Performance Indicators (KPIs)/measures of success/how do we know it's having an impact on profitability?

The first question seems obvious but actually isn't. HR can tend to get caught up in justifying its existence by designing many bureaucratic processes, over-involving itself or launching many random 'flavour of the month' initiatives that can leave people feeling confused, fed up and even angry. It's as if HR is bored with its lot and feels a need to come up with new ideas to remind people of just how worthwhile it is.

The second question centres around your financial impact on the business and yet again HR can often be its own worst enemy. Performance indicators that only HR are interested in do not endear you to the people within the business.

I'll help you answer these two questions in the forthcoming lessons.

In the meantime, put it all together so far and you have this:

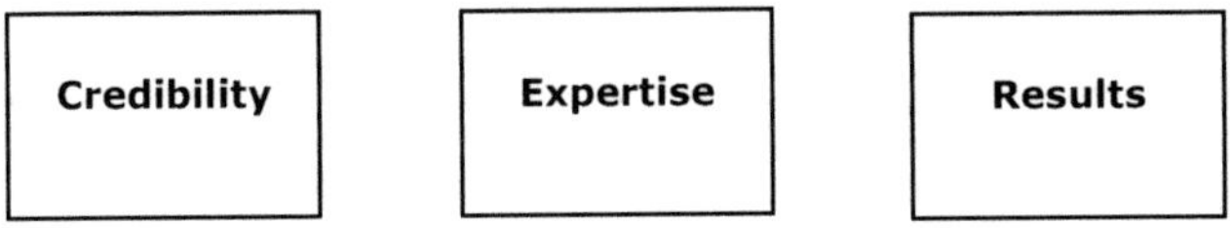

Credibility	**Expertise**	**Results**

Put in another way: credibility, expertise and results give you **IMPACT** in the business.

As you will see, the three are often interlinked. Credibility can come through results or demonstrating expertise and the need for results can spur you on to develop your expertise.

This book is about approaching HR from a business mindset and raising your level of influence and impact to improve the fortunes of your company.

The other lessons here all contain tactics, pieces of advice and skills to master that should all go into your 'toolkit'. A helpful summary is also included from lesson three onwards to help you understand some of the main points made.

You may not agree with everything written here, it may be that some of my points instead just provoke thought. I hope, however, that you can take as much on board as possible to help shape and determine your own approach to HR.

So let's get on with it …

LESSON 2
THE HR GENERALIST ROLE

The generalist HR professional should always be ensuring that the job is centered around:

1) the expertise and tasks required within the HR role description and the function itself, as appropriate

2) what the business wants — ask them

3) fitting and linking activities to the company's strategy, aims and objectives

4) activities linked to legal and other compliance requirements.

It is probably a fair statement to say that, nowadays, HR is fundamentally about three things:

1) getting the best out of people (Performance)

2) getting at least what is required from people (Productivity)

3) having the right resource in the right place (Efficiency).

Breaking this down further quite simply or callously, depending on how you view it, HR is concerned with:

1) getting people into the business

2) maximising the performance of people

3) developing them to meet their career aspirations and matching these to what the business needs

4) moving them out (be it from their choice, the business choosing or other circumstances).

Bringing People In

Everyone wants to attract and recruit the best people they can get their hands on. This is increasingly gaining in importance because of the all important 'War for Talent' you've probably heard of or read about.

Recruitment uses the company brand to attract people and activities you could be involved with or manage would include:

– designing and running assessment centres

– developing recruitment processes

– determining factors such as pay and reward

– managing the advertising campaign

– managing response

– interviewing

– testing

– associated administration

– dealing with recruitment agencies.

What you are always ultimately trying to do is gain competitive advantage here to select the best and differentiate in your approach where possible.

Maximising Performance

The HR role plays a strong part in fostering and encouraging competitiveness between people to improve results — that's a long way from the 'welfare' manager bit isn't it? But it is also about being the voice of reason who can deal with the things that frustrate employees and help get them back on track whilst enabling the managers to run their businesses and maximise performance.

This part is also about how businesses use the 'carrot and stick' approach:

- Use of incentives
- How people are motivated to increase performance through financial and non financial means
- The nature of welfare and support
- Training your managers to be great bosses
- Getting the right management styles
- The use of discipline, how you bring people back into line and correct poor performance
- Dealing with employee relations/legal issues

Developing Them

- What training is on offer?
- How do you close skill gaps?
- How do you get successors lining up for the jobs so that the business is not left with gaping holes?
- What are you doing to develop tomorrow's leaders?
- What does the business need a year or more from now and how is the business changing?

Moving Them On

Nothing is forever and sooner or later people need to leave the business but it is obviously better if good people will stay.

- How are you stopping good people from leaving?
- How are you reducing the costs of unnecessary employee turnover?
- How do you protect the business from legal claims from disgruntled leavers?
- How up to date are you with employment law and how well have you upskilled the management team?

And all the activities above need to be taken on with the appropriate focus on cost.

There are also all of the activities that are internal to the HR function, be it administration or payroll activity for example. Other specialisms will also play a part e.g. diversity and welfare. The level you operate at and the type of business you work in will determine how involved you are in these latter elements as well as the more strategic 'business partner' stuff.

So, this pretty much adds up to one stark goal:

Wanting the most out of people for your money — all at odds with that traditional welfare role isn't it?

Let's be clear, HR should now be a mean machine and many of the activities above are not an exact science. Everyone has their opinion of what should be happening because some of the activities I have listed apply at one point or another to everybody! This is another peculiar issue that is somewhat unique to HR in business; everyone has an opinion on what would motivate them, what training they SHOULD be having etc. and much of this may be at odds with what the business wants to do. People would obviously have less of an idea of the technology required to improve a telecoms system in a company or even an opinion around it! Working in IT must be easier then, yes? (Ok, perhaps not!)

Because HR activities directly affect people the risks of the message being misconstrued or activities getting a bad press are always going to be heightened. It should make you more cautious and determined to get things right and continuously ensuring that all angles have been covered before your output is 'out there'. It's not about 'spin', more so it's about doing the courtesy of putting your feet in others' shoes and giving things full consideration.

LESSON 3
IT'S ALL ABOUT GETTING RESULTS

So this is what it's all ultimately about. It's also one of the most annoying things about HR to other people: the lack of tangibility, of hard results that can be measured and judged.

Before we look at how HR links to company strategy let's consider from the 'bottom up' what should be happening with the business or business unit you support.

Firstly, if everything was easy then everybody would be doing it well and that's where HR can often fall short. Measures or KPIs (Key Performance Indicators), where used, often bear no real relation to what the business wants in terms of helping deliver the overall bottom line results. Getting the right indicators is a difficult exercise that needs a good deal of consideration and collaboration with others.

As an example, you may be all for measuring and looking to improve your absence rates because it 'feels' higher than the national norm. Let's say it's averaging 5% and you want to get it down to 3%. Now, this is a great measure that can have a great impact on productivity, morale, costs and so on. But if it isn't that important to the main stakeholders (line managers, top management etc.) then you are never really going to get that far with achieving the target. On the other hand, you may achieve the target but no one really cares as they feel there are more important things to worry about!

It is therefore critical that your targets and objectives align to what the business wants to achieve. In turn, the business needs to understand HOW you can positively IMPACT results through your role.

At this point you may be thinking: 'so everything I do has to be only what the managers want?'

Well, No!

You see, you're an expert and it's your job to help the business understand the impact of low absence (in this example) on the business.

You should be able to tangibly articulate what the effects and impact would be:

For Example :

A 2% reduction in absence = 100 days extra attendance by employees.

Generally, 60% of these 100 days has to be covered by other workers at an additional cost of £20,000 a year.

On top of that is the intangible cost of lower morale because of the burden placed on colleagues which may in turn affect their productivity.

On top of that you can factor in the administration around sickness absence, return to work interviews, medical referrals, etc.

As you can see, a compelling argument is already being made to focus on absence reduction as a key measure for the business.

By making this case you are helping others understand the wider impact of detrimental things that could happen in the business which may directly impact the company's ability to make money.

Further tangible arguments could be made with a whole host of important measures:

- Rate of employee turnover (people leaving)
- Staff satisfaction measurement
- Success of the company management succession plan
- Number of employees receiving an appraisal or review
- Percentage of jobs filled internally

...and so on.

The important things to consider are:

1) Does the business understand what this measure is all about?

2) Can I articulate tangibly how the measure can improve the fortunes of the business?

3) Is the measure trackable — can we see how far we have come?

4) Is this something that managers will then buy into, believe in and want to deliver?

The last point is all important as you may be the expert when it comes to these measures but it is the people in the business that will be ultimately instrumental in helping to achieve the target.

Most businesses now have a raft of 'People' activities and plans within their strategies. Often, these are developed with HR Directors who are well placed to help the key decision makers understand the people measures that can most influence overall performance.

This can therefore help make the HR role a lot easier as you are able to align your priorities and targets closely to what the business requires.

In terms of the dreaded words 'adding value', once you are clear on how you are impacting the business in terms of traditional HR activities, you can then also move on to use your expertise in areas that at first sight may not look like they are linked to HR.

For example, improving operational efficiency in terms of what people do is all important. There may be frontline activities that you don't really *understand* in terms of the detail but may be operating inefficiently.

For example, there may be too many checkout operators in a retail business. The HR role can help objectively identify the issues and then the solutions required. For example:

- the peaks and troughs of customer flow
- how resource can be reallocated elsewhere at quieter times
- the legal framework if having to reduce numbers of overall staff.

These activities can have an even more direct and tangible impact on the business but the nature of your involvement would again come back to the level of credibility and expertise that you have within the business.

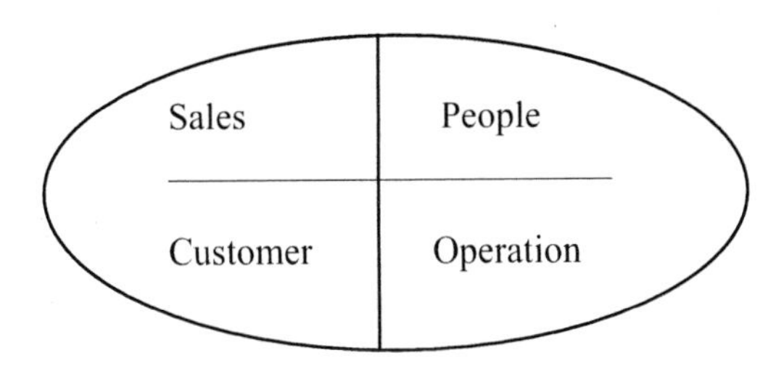

In recent years, the *Balanced Scorecard* has been much in evidence.

This consists of a number of key measures in business that will be focused around financial, operational, service and people related targets, to name a few.

The Scorecard expects that employees keep these targets front of mind and that their own activities be linked to the targets as appropriate.

This ensures that there is less 'preference over priority' in terms of what people do day-to-day and that they balance their time around the measures that ultimately matter.

There are various texts for HR people that focus on the Balanced Scorecard approach and familiarisation with this now can give you a great head start in HR.

Anyway, I digress slightly: By now you'll hopefully have a clear understanding of the importance of linking what you do to what the business wants to do to improve performance. You'll also understand that it is your expertise that helps the business understand the impact that other people activities can have on the bottom line.

Company goals	**Goals of the business unit you support**	**Your plans and activities that support these goals**

When it comes to company goals, the trick is to try and link these into what the business unit you support is trying to achieve (hopefully this itself links to the company goals). You are then working with your managers to come up with plans and activities to support their goals and go some way to achieving what the company is looking for.

Example:

Company goal – Improve internal succession planning to retain and grow own talent

Business unit goal – Ensure there is one internal successor behind each role above grade 4

HR activity – Identification of successor with line managers, identify and close skills gaps, address any other issues around pay and motivation that may be impeding internal succession.

But you also work within the HR function and, like other departments, there are a number of areas internal to the HR team that can attract its own KPIs.

For example, how much is each external recruit costing in terms of agency fees, administration, management time etc. This key measure (cost per hire) is important because the HR role is also concerned with keeping costs under control and improving its own efficiency.

What about administration? How much resource is being tied up in unnecessary activity, e.g. if you regularly take up three references on new employees, why not take two?

What about the number of complaints or tribunal applications? Have these come as a result of poor processes and procedures that could have been avoided?

These measures are often attached to the 'routine' of HR and are often not as 'sexy' or interesting but nevertheless are a good indicator of how commercially aware and credible you are as an HR professional. You have to practice what you preach and improving the performance of the business goes hand in hand with driving performance within your own internal function.

Summary

- Targets and measures can be divided into those linked to company strategy and those linked to the efficiency of the HR function itself.
- The measures need to be as tangible as possible to be able to clearly identify the impact on the business.
- It's your job to help managers and employees understand what the measures and targets are all about and their effects. It's your expertise that then helps them deliver against them.

- To get you into the flow of this, here are some other example Key Performance Indicators or measures:
  - ➢ Effectiveness of training — impact on service, financial indicators etc.
  - ➢ Degree that people feel involved in decision making within the business
  - ➢ Diversity — make up of workforce
  - ➢ Success rate of external hires
  - ➢ Time gap between vacancy and offer of employment
  - ➢ Number of training days
  - ➢ Improvement rate of poor performers
- The HR function itself also needs to be efficient and maximising its own internal performance.

Lesson 4

The Power of Three

Effective prioritising for better problem solving

In my experience, when people are asked to describe an issue or problem they face, often the reply is made up of 'thick fog' full of different points of view and parts of a problem that either overlap or go off at tangents and it can all become quite confusing.

For example:

Asked why one colleague doesn't get on with another, the answer may be made up of 22 different components, such as the history between the two individuals, what has happened recently, other people's involvement and so on. It's therefore very difficult to get to the root of the issue and help with solutions.

As another example, ask a manager what they consider to be the cause of someone's poor performance and again you may get various vague assumptions, recent examples of where things have gone wrong, manifestations of a bit of prejudice or stereotyping on the manager's part and finally some concrete factual points! It's all very 'foggy' and you can then begin to understand why the performance hasn't been managed effectively before.

The HR professional has to have a lot of these 'diagnosis' conversations because they are often not 'on the floor' everyday and obviously will not know what is going on with people in any great detail (unless of course your remit only covers a small number of people). Often, the managers themselves are too close to a situation and find it hard to stand back with objectivity and really consider what is going on.

The Top Three's

My 'Power of Three' pretty much falls out of that old favourite: Pareto's Law, better known as 'The 80/20 Rule'. This states that if you focus on the right 20% it will give you an 80% return. This is as opposed to devoting time to lots of other things that feel important but aren't really going to help you achieve what you need to, or as quickly and effectively.

In an HR context, it simply involves encouraging people to speak and consider things in terms of 'The Top Three's':

For example, consider:

- what three things would you change about him if you could to get better performance?
- what three things would give you the greatest chance of achieving a sales target?
- what three things would make her a better manager?
- what are the three things that most frustrate other people about that colleague?

It enables you to understand and prioritise:

1) root causes to issues and

2) the solution — what needs to happen first with reference to what will give the greatest payback or return.

Doesn't everybody think like this?

Well, it sounds really simple but it isn't practiced in reality. Given the chance, people will download lots of things because they are frustrated and are 'venting'. It is very difficult for anyone to help people like this and, if allowed, usually results in what I call 'Tabloid Headlines'.

Tabloid Headlines

These are the generalisations that people make. For example, one person may have left a department due to relocation and then be followed by another who has gone for family reasons. The tabloid headline that some will scream out is:

'Morale causes exodus from sinking ship'

'Terrible manager forcing good people out!'

There will always be people in business and teams who love to read, spread and deliver bad news — true or not. Whilst there may be elements of truth that the HR professional needs to get under the skin of, so there will also be a raft of distracting and unhelpful 'gossip' that does not improve a situation.

By thinking in 'Top Three's' and asking 'Top Three' questions you are better equipped to get past 'tabloid headlines' and understand the reality of a situation. This should help prevent you from focusing on something that's actual priority ranking is number 17 but it is the 'tabloid' headlines that have forced you wrongly to deal with the point right now!

For example, in the scenario above where two people are leaving a department you may have heard the tabloid whispers that the manager is terrible and has to go. You could take this at face value and confront the manager (or advise that the manager be confronted) who could be quite innocent in all this. Alternatively, one of your top three priorities may be to understand the reasons for leaving as it may turn out that none of it is to do with the workplace or the boss.

If a manager is telling you how terrible everything is and how the company is going backwards then ask them to consider the three things they dislike most. By doing this it helps the individual realise that not everything is bad and that it is only three things (or 20% of all of his issues) that are having probably 80% of the negative impact. Addressing these three things through action or explanation can obviously help turn things around in terms of their perception of the business and how things are going.

The mind thinks clearly in 'threes' very easily and logically. This book itself is based on three key pillars: credibility, expertise and results. Stories have three elements: a beginning, middle and end.

If you gave someone a list of five aspects of their behaviour that they needed to develop, they would then, more than likely, be able to choose the three aspects that they agreed with most or were easiest to address. I believe that people have a hard time balancing lots of pieces of information in their heads and that dealing in three's can help clearly separate things out. It helps people to prioritise and reduce stress levels.

The HR function and Top Three's

You can also use Top Three's in your own role:

- What are the Top Three HR Key Performance Indicators (KPIs) that would have most impact on the business?
- What Top Three things can I do to reduce administration?

Identifying the Right Top Three's

It is all very well being able to pick three things but are they the right ones? Some of this is about having the talent to be able to get to the heart of issues very quickly and identify the wins. Some tips that can help include:

1) Drawing on past experience – When a particular priority was worked on previously did it have a lasting and successful impact or did the issue still continue?

2) Analysis – Model different options open to you to understand the effect each one will have. For example, ten teams may have high employee turnover but use statistics to help understand which three should be focused on for the greatest effect.

3) Listening to others – You may have a fixed opinion but there will be other subject matter experts who will be

closer to a situation and can help identify priorities with you.

Identifying the *right* 'Top Three' of anything is a skill that comes with practice and experience. Developing the skill boosts your credibility because you will get to the solutions to issues quicker and help people deal with underlying issues in a much more effective way.

It will help you get past the 'fog' of a situation and help others see things more clearly.

Summary

- Focusing on 'Top Three's' can often help untangle issues to help come to the right decisions and solutions
- See through the 'tabloid headlines' to get to the heart of an issue by focusing on the important things rather than what is being potentially 'seized on' by others.
- Develop your skill around picking the right Top Three by drawing on past experience, good analysis and listening to others' perspectives and opinions.

Lesson 5
Back to the Floor
Stand back before you take aim!

'Ground floor, please'

It is always difficult in any new role to stand back and assess the environment around you, including issues, opportunities etc. The tendency for most people is to want to get stuck into the priorities and to get as many quick wins under their belt as possible.

However, you always need to be able to take an objective and reflective view of things in a new role before you get too assimilated into the culture and caught up in other agendas and other's potentially political activities!

Going back to the floor

One of the most effective things you can do in the very early days is to go 'back to the floor' (or simply go to 'the floor' if you have never seen it before!). This can have a number of benefits:

1) It can really boost your credibility in the vital weeks where no one really knows you but people have their own expectations and perceptions.

2) It can help your commercial decision-making when settling into your role as you are then more aware of the detail behind issues, problems and opportunities.

So what does this involve?

Simply, you can break the activity into a number of goals to achieve that will give it real purpose:

- Shadow people in a variety of roles to understand not just what they do but also to find out how they feel about their role, the obstacles they face and what they would do to overcome them if they were in charge.

This therefore also becomes a listening exercise and can often determine 'quick wins'. People often waste no time in wanting to tell you where things are going wrong and how they can be improved. This is even more so when the individual sees you as someone who can actually help make change happen. The worst thing at this point is to make promises or 'noises' about things you are going to do when you are too early into the role and still trying to understand the nature and degree of your own influence in the business.

Giving the idea that you can 'wave a magic wand' in an attempt to gain credibility can often backfire if promises are not subsequently delivered.

- If you can, try and undertake activities within some of the main roles. There is no substitute for actually stepping in someone else's shoes.

This probably does not happen enough. Most people only want an awareness of the 'operation' and would rather spend the time asking questions, listening and making notes. However, actually carrying out the role really does put you in someone else's skin. This is subtly different because the degree to which you will understand complexities, obstacles, issues etc. is greater when you can experience things for yourself at first hand.

You may even want to or need to undertake some of the actual training that those in the role have to go through themselves.

This gives you the other benefit of being able to experience how good the content and delivery of training is and whether you as a trainee feel you have benefited from it.

- Build in time in the coming weeks and months to revisit some of these people so you can understand recurring issues and how things have possibly moved forward for them.

Very beneficial but often quite risky, this in some ways is an evaluation exercise. If you have promised changes that you know you can influence then it is worthwhile to be able to see the impact of these and understand how they have improved things (or not!). The second obvious benefit in revisiting the roles some weeks later is that you develop the relationships with others and again this can only reflect well when it comes to your perceived credibility.

Quick wins

So far I have highlighted the need for a period of observation and reflection that needs to go hand in hand with whatever quick wins you can tick off in your early weeks. But how do you define a quick win? You may think that something is a quick win but when you get into it and strip back the layers there is actually more to it and it now requires a six month project! This is why you have to be very careful with attempts to 'tick things off' in your early weeks. Act with extreme caution and only proceed when you know there are no other issues, agendas or conflicts around the activity that are going to make things a bit more protracted.

Quick wins – Example

One of the team managers has phoned you in your first week to say that one of the team is due a pay rise and your predecessor had just not got round to processing it. They are asking for you to co-ordinate the paperwork for the next day as the individual is not happy and will leave otherwise!

So what do you do?

This is a very common example of something you can be faced with in your early days into the role.

Options:

1) Process the paperwork, individual is happy and manager believes you to be very responsive. Seems like a good win / win.

2) Review the pay policy and meet with the manager to go through rules and criteria ahead of then agreeing what the pay proposal should be for sign off at the required level.

3) Ask your manager (or the line manager's manager) why they think the pay rise probably did not get processed previously.

Option 1 is an example of a quick win that can quickly backfire. You don't really have enough information other than the manager's word who could be 'pulling the wool over your eyes' and taking advantage of your being new to the role.

Option 2 is worthwhile but actually could become quite a lengthy, drawn out process for an individual who is on the verge of leaving as they have probably had to wait a while already.

There is also the 'red tape' label that you could get early on from others who see you as an obstacle.

Option 3 is the best idea. Seems obvious but your manager or someone else may have better, more factual and objective information as to why the pay increase hasn't been processed. There may be issues with the individual, the line manager may have promised them something that they haven't the authority to deliver. Finding this out for yourself ensures that the right decision is made without comeback. It also shows the line manager that you are no pushover but equally are not going to draw something out for longer than it needs to be.

See what I mean about 'quick wins'? – They often aren't!

If the early days are about identifying and going back to the floor and achieving quick wins, what else do you need to concentrate on?

The Routines

What are they, what is the Service Level Agreement (SLA) in terms of what needs to be done, by when and to what standard? The routines are all important in HR because there is no point in getting onto bigger things if the day-to-day routines just haven't happened or aren't happening.

Type these routines up and divide them into daily, weekly, monthly, quarterly and ad hoc. Keep them at the front of a file pocket folder so that they are front of mind until they are embedded and become second nature to you.

Later on you can use tools like the '80/20 principle' to determine how effective these routines are and whether or not they can be reduced or changed to achieve the same outcome.

The Strategy

What is the business strategy in this company?

How does HR play a role here in delivering strategy?

How much of the strategy is reflected in the routines I am observing and how much is instead focused on meatier activities or projects?

Example

The **strategy**: The business wants to improve its sales by attracting better calibre, higher skilled individuals externally.

a) What **routines** do you observe: How effective is the recruitment process in terms of the steps followed, paperwork and key activities so that the candidate is getting the right service?

There is no point having great initiatives or projects in this area if you can't get the routines right when it comes to the recruitment administration throughout the process to offer stage and beyond.

b) The **'meatier bits'** you observe: projects, initiatives etc.

How effective are these in terms of attracting and recruiting great people? What success has been had so far? What has worked well and not so well? Who are the stakeholders? Who has been involved? Are new ideas needed, is there enough money?

All are valid questions to be considering in the early days when assessing current activities against their impact on the overall business strategy.

With your findings you can then build a SWOT analysis:

<u>Strengths</u>

E.g. Recruitment campaign and PR is resulting in a steady number of good candidates applying.

Weaknesses

The lead time in responding to candidates at different parts of the process.

Opportunities

What about starting headhunting activity internally with pre-identified individuals who are good at it?

Threats

The higher pay rates being offered elsewhere.

The SWOT analysis can help 'funnel' the right activities for the future. Notice you are not running off and doing all of these things right now. It is about evaluating 'how things are going' at this stage before you agree on and get to the right priorities.

Standing back – other considerations

- Who has the real influence? Who do you need to get buy in from? Understand this early on to avoid wasted effort in the future.
- Do you have all the information you need? Is it being withheld for some reason? Are there 'you don't need to see that' elements from others!? Question this closely.
- Also, consider **Lesson 6** 'Do anything asked of you' and add this to your approach in the early days to your role.

Summary

- Don't rush off to achieve lots of things in your early weeks. Have a structure and activities that take into account:
    - going back to the floor
    - achieving the right quick wins
- understanding the routines
- getting an understanding of whether HR activities are buying into and linked to the business strategy
- knowing who to influence and who has influence
- having the right information to help you with decision making and planning
- **Lesson 6** – 'Do anything asked of you in the beginning.'

LESSON 6

DO ANYTHING ASKED OF YOU IN THE BEGINNING — THEN 'PUSH BACK'

' The CIPD didn't say anything about having to do this in HR!'

As you can see by now, HR often has to deal with others' perceptions of the function and what it does or doesn't achieve.

When starting out in your first generalist role, it is tempting to want to assert yourself from the beginning. This may involve wanting to be clear with others about what you will and won't do and accept, or you may have the urge to want to set your own ground rules, particularly with line managers.

However, HR does not directly manage any of these managers and nobody really has to do anything you advise or call for as your level of influence will generally be quite low at the beginning.

It is critical that you build credibility as soon as possible — any mistakes made at the beginning will not be forgotten by the line and will only serve to enforce any negative stereotypes or assumptions that some may have of HR.

So...

Do Some Dirty Work!

Now this may be an unpopular view but I have always found it to work successfully and have rarely been proved wrong in my own experience.

Basically, this can involve:

- Perhaps doing something menial for a line manager — writing a letter for them that they should do themselves or having a conversation with one of their people that they don't want to have!

- Allowing them to take a course of action that they would normally expect HR to 'veto' and disallow for being too risky.

Activities such as these break down any perception that HR is an obstacle and of low value and can actively help build rapport and develop a relationship with others. It feels to the other person that you really are practical, commercially aware, trying to help them and living in reality rather than the ideal world they may think you live in.

Of course, you're not really doing anything of any real value at all. It's all part of your plan!

Example Activity from HR:

1) HR writes a letter for a manager who is too busy to do it himself and its about 'people things' anyway.

2) HR holds a training needs analysis meeting with a manager's direct report, even though the manager should do it.

Manager's perception: HR are really helpful, not as bad as everyone thinks and can really free up your time.

HR's reality: This is just reactionary, hand holding, allowing managers to abdicate and only really ever keeping them reliant on you because you haven't equipped them to do things for themselves.

The problem here is that this type of relationship, if it continued past a point, can be likened to that of a drug addict and the 'pusher'!

You are trying to boost your credibility and give the answers to managers or make it as easy as possible for them. Your belief here is that they will then rate you and be compliant when you need them to do certain activities. The reality, however, is that the more you over support them the more dependent on you they become as they can't do things for themselves.

A drug pusher makes an addict feel better and continues supplying drugs to make the addict feel continuously satisfied. The point comes when you stop giving drugs and withdrawal symptoms set in. In my example, you have over supported the manager so they then actually fall behind other managers when it comes to skill level and find it difficult to cope with some situations or issues. The whole exercise is counter productive in the end if you have pushed it too far and there is over reliance on you.

Remember the **expertise** point too. You may be getting grateful comments from managers but you are not really using your expertise.

Example of a REAL & VALUABLE HR Activity that will support the manager:

Manager to carry out a training needs analysis with one of their staff

This is an example of an HR Activity that uses expertise. It may be more difficult but ultimately upskills manager so they can do it for themselves:

So, train the manager in how to carry out a training needs analysis exercise so that they are continuously aware of the need to always be developing direct reports. The activity also helps the manager understand why there may be gaps in performance and how to identify them.

This helps the manager to ultimately be able to fend for themselves, but of course it's a fine balance. Sometimes you will have to do things that the manager cannot do, e.g. legal activities or salary benchmarking activity, because you have more tools, resources or expertise at your disposal than they have.

This upskilling and 'fending for yourself' point is evident within other functions. In Finance, for example, the accountants will produce profit and loss accounts for managers. It is for the managers, however, to take actions based on the information. Finance can help them interpret it but it would not make sense for them to tell the manager every last detail of what he/she should now do to boost profitability. The manager has to build their own financial awareness skills so that they can make their own decisions. You can teach someone how to play the piano but that person ultimately has to then play it for themselves!

If the manager has developed expertise and can deliver results in a timely fashion then the business will be thankful that you have influenced effectively and upskilled them so early on.

In my experience, I have seen many HR professionals new to a role make critical mistakes:

- Asserting their position by being clear that they will not do things for managers that the latter should do for themselves. The HR individual thinks this makes them appear strong and true to what HR should really be doing and focusing its energies on. To managers, it looks like another person on top of their own boss who is also giving them a hard time!
- Telling managers that any advice given to them by HR is just that - advice! Any course of action then taken by the manager is indeed a management decision and the consequences are theirs, and not yours! (More of this in **Lesson 9**).
- Compelling managers to follow 'best practices' without first understanding the obstacles that managers face.
- Making assumptions without really knowing how the business operates.

Many of the lessons in this book can help prevent mistakes when new to the HR role. Doing some 'dirty work' at the beginning can lessen the impact of any mistakes that come later. People are quicker to forgive when they have already started to develop a good relationship with you.

Freeing up time – a key HR intention

At different points in my career I have talked with managers about the need to free up their time and how I can help do this. It always gets a great response because there never seems to be enough hours in the day to do everything a business may demand of people. Freeing up time also allows individuals to concentrate more on the activities that should ultimately achieve better results.

You always therefore need to ask yourself the question:

Will my activity ultimately free up *more* time for people in the long term?

The more someone perceives you have freed up their time over the long term, the greater the influence you will have with them.

But isn't this a contradiction? Surely if I continue doing all of these simple, low value things for them then I have freed up their time haven't I?

No, and that is the critical bit to understand. Carrying out reactive, relatively simple low value activities for managers or other individuals in the short term only frees up *as much time as that task takes to complete.* There are then better ways to free up far more time in the future.

For example: A manager needs to write a presentation for his team meeting that focuses in on the key responsibilities of his direct reports. You think it's a good idea as it will help improve overall performance. The manager isn't sure how to use PowerPoint and so you help out by writing the presentation for him.

Sounds simple! You have freed up his time and told yourself that it's all for the good and an effective team meeting will now be held as a result.

However, if you arrange for the manager to then have PowerPoint training you have given him a new skill and the ability to be able to do this himself. This will free up more time for him in the future because you may not always be there. What if you are on holiday and he has to do another presentation? His added stress levels and his need to get someone else to write the presentation is only going to be more time consuming for him (especially if he can't get anyone to do it!)

It's the same if you are having the difficult conversations with his direct reports that he should be having himself.

If he was 'nipping things in the bud' and having his own conversations, in the right way and at the right time then it would reduce his having to sort out more difficult, time consuming situations later on when things are left to escalate! Upskilling the manager to be able to deal with these things will save infinitely more time in the future because difficult people management situations will have reduced or be resolved more effectively.

The other point to make here is that doing these sorts of low value things for the individual doesn't free up your time to focus on the more analytical, higher level, higher results activities that could really make a difference for the manager. This is covered in **Lesson 10**. For example, you could spend time firefighting employee turnover issues for the manager or use the time to analyse why it is happening and help design long term solutions to resolve the issues once and for all.

The cut off point – So when can I then start to 'push back' with managers?

You only need to do 'the dirty work' a few times with each individual to find that you have gone some way to earning their respect. You may even find that comparisons are made between you and your predecessor in your favour. As much as it feels that you shouldn't have to do this, it really does make your job easier in the medium term and beyond because it actually helps develop your influence.

Doing some 'dirty work' shouldn't therefore last long. You need to intuitively find the point with each person whereby enough is enough and you now need to move on to delivering your role as it should be to give long term benefits rather than a short term 'quick shot in the arm'.

This can be subtly achieved in a number of ways:

1) Begin to challenge more and more in the conversations you are having with the other person, bringing into play your expertise.

2) Use humour appropriately to defuse any possible tensions as you 'push back' more.

3) Bargain with the other person — 'I can do this for you if you can do this for me'.

4) Outwardly upskill the manager/employee so they are more self sufficient and do not always look to you for answers or help.

This may all appear to be quite manipulative — and it is, towards a good outcome for all! It's something anyone new to a role can do to win co-operation and respect from others but it is even more invaluable within the HR role. Remember that trust and confidentiality are all important, particularly when you are dealing with high risk situations. Credibility is key.

Don't be a pushover but do 'give' a bit more than you normally would in these early days. It makes a lot of the lessons in this book even easier to implement as you get into your role.

Summary

- Do some 'dirty work' for the manager in the short term – take on low value activities they should be doing themselves.
- Always ask yourself – 'Are my activities supporting the manager to free up their own time, and more of it in the long term – or does it only free it up in the short term?'
- Free up your own time to concentrate on the higher value activities that give real long terms benefits to the manager.
- Know when the 'cut off' point has been reached to be able to start 'pushing back' with the manager.

LESSON 7
DO YOUR DUTY!
Welfare & Ethics

If you study any function within your business, be it Marketing, Finance, IT etc. you will discover that there are certain 'duty' factors inherently present.

The 'duty' factor

If a Police Officer is driving a squad car and spots someone driving somewhat dangerously then they will, in all likelihood, pull them over. Why do they do this? They are not bonused for every single arrest they make and probably all they can hope for is a bit of recognition back at the station!

Police Officers sign up to 'do their duty' when they join the force. It is their duty to detect and prevent crime and if they turn too much of a blind eye then this duty will become diluted. It could also lead to an increase in crime if enough Police Officers are doing the same thing!

How does this work in the world of business? Well, each job role has its own set of duties ascribed to it. These will vary in levels of responsibility and accountability but are present nonetheless.

Each function also has its own duties. Marketing has a duty to develop and protect the company's brand and its image. Finance has a duty to look after the numbers for the financial wellbeing of the business.

When things go wrong in this area or rules are flouted then it is ultimately for the managers and directors within these functions to stamp down and restore order and equilibrium.

So HR has its own duties too which can involve a number of difficult trade offs that may affect your credibility and how HR is perceived.

HR's duty

It is tempting for others to consider that HR's potential lack of tangibility can mean that there is a lack of accountability or few real duties within the function.

With reference to the other lessons in this book it is clear, however, that the more tangible and relevant you can make HR then the more its duties will be respected.

In line with your job role you need to:

- protect the business from legal risks or potential claims from disgruntled employees
- be a moral guardian for what is right and wrong in terms of how people are managed and motivated
- help people to understand and cope with change
- ensure that decisions made around people (from recruitment selection to pay reviews etc.) are justified (see **Lesson 8**)
- ensure a consistent and ethical approach to people matters.

All of the above can be viewed as serious 'duties'. When you see things that are wrong or are contrary to the duty then it is for HR to stand up, highlight the issue and work to resolve it.

The theme from the beginning of this book is that there can be a perception that it's all just 'people stuff' and anyone can do it — right?

This is a dangerous approach to take because if every influential person in the business did what they wanted to then it wouldn't be long before some of the duties described above are disregarded.

It's also a Key Performance Indicator results thing. If you do not do your duty and call things to account when appropriate then ultimately business results could be adversely impacted.

If a manager is allowed to continuously bully employees then the latter will leave and employee turnover increases with all the associated costs of re-hiring, training etc.

The 'Welfare' bit – 'Weep and Sweep!'

'Got an issue? Here's a tissue!'

Many years ago HR was called 'Staff Management'. It then became 'Personnel' in the 1980s and 1990s and has evolved more recently into 'Human Resources'. None of the words are particularly exciting and few of them sum up what HR really does. I have even heard Human Resources renamed 'Human Remains' in some quarters and so there is clearly a PR issue here!

However, as HR has become seemingly more strategic so the perception has arisen that the human, emotional element has been lost in businesses and that HR people are not doing anything to change this.

People often have a view of what HR should be doing though, and if you talk to anyone on the 'shop floor' you will often hear the following statements:

'HR should be looking after the staff'

'Welfare falls under HR'

'HR are just on management's side, not ours'

..and so on.

We can clearly see then, from a shopfloor perspective, that a traditional view definitely exists around HR needing to be the 'people's champion'. So have things got worst over the years in that respect. Yes. Probably!

HR has developed as a profession. People entering it are looking more to specialise, think strategically and engage in meaty activities so there is often little room here for the 'employee advocate' or welfare role so prevalent in its roots and history.

Often, HR is supporting the management agenda and things can feel too weighted towards this and so it results in HR becoming effectively another line manager to individuals. HR people themselves often have their own phrases that do nothing to promote this, some of them unprintable here but one of them typically being:

'Weep and Sweep'!

Effectively, give someone a few minutes to get something off their chest, give them a few well meaning words and then let them get on with it so you can focus on more strategic, business facing activities!!

Am I cynical? Probably.

Anyone in the profession taking too long with this or genuinely trying to help somebody is accused of being 'fluffy' and reinforcing the negative stereotype of HR. Anyone 'sweeping' quickly is seen as highly commercial with a 'no nonsense' attitude.

But there is surely a middle ground to be occupied? So where does welfare and ethics come into play?

The commercial context

Many businesses now are using 'employer branding' activities increasingly as a way of helping to win the 'war for talent'. Basically, too many competitors and not enough good people out there. As businesses look to differentiate themselves, concepts like welfare and ethics can become prominent as a way of attracting good people.

For example, the benefits offered by a business may include improved healthcare coverage to include proactive medical 'MOT's', there may be progressive work/life balance policies or onsite massage facilities! All of these, whilst appearing gimmicky, all go some way to demonstrate the importance of employee welfare. Furthermore, attraction brochures may talk of the high standards and principles within the business and how ethics play a strong part and extend to the promotion of great equal opportunity practices.

The legal context

The role of welfare and ethics also forms part of what today is called the 'psychological contract' between employer and employee. These are the perceptions around what obligations should exist between each other.

One of the catch all legal claims in employment law is the breach by an employer of the duty around 'trust and confidence'. If you like, there has potentially been a fundamental breakdown in the psychological contract.

Much of this can come down to how employees are treated, how decisions are arrived at and how certain standards and principles have been applied.

The operational context

Perceived injustices and an uncaring attitude contribute to employee de-motivation. This is inevitably going to lead to increased employee turnover which will itself affect the day-to-day running of the business. It also affects morale which in turn can influence productivity.

Welfare and ethics isn't 'fluffy', it's not a distraction or a nice thing to do that is irrelevant to modern HR. As is one of the themes of this book, it's about partnering with the business rather than being the sole person that employees come to when they have issues and problems. In some ways, you should be their last port of call in this area if the manager is upskilled and aware of their responsibilities. It can sometimes be a failure if the individual has to come to you; the manager may have abdicated somewhere or have been ill equipped to deal with the issue.

A good rule of thumb is to adopt the following when considering your duties and the role of welfare and ethics in supporting people management:

Your decision making prompt card

Example:

Sarah is in a pressured sales role and has a degenerative disease – Should we let her work full time from home?

Considerations

- Duty to consider 'reasonable adjustments' to accommodate what is probably a disability.

- Sarah wants to still be around people rather than permanently at home but suffers mainly in the mornings.
- She may be able to achieve more, however it will be more difficult to communicate with the team and she would go on less client visits as a result of being at home.

Solution

Work three days at home, two days in office with days in office starting on a later shift. Adjust targets slightly if sales dip. Review monthly to see whether we can still justify adjustments being made against the need to achieve a certain sales target.

Here, the focus is on trying to do the right thing for Sarah as she is in a difficult situation but ensuring that if the impact on the business becomes too adverse then the arrangement may need reviewing.

This solution therefore addresses the legal, business, welfare and moral questions raised as a result of Sarah's unfortunate situation.

Summary

- There are a number of duties unique to the HR role in terms of being the moral guardian and questioning the ethics and justification of decisions made that affect people.
- HR has a key role in promoting and looking after the welfare interests of individuals in the business.
- Welfare and ethics affect the success or otherwise of business strategy and the day-to-day operation.
- Decision making should be mindful of the legal context, the impact on people, the impact on the operation and the role HR should play because of its expertise and the resources it can draw on.

LESSON 8
THINK ABOUT IT
Flexibility, commercial decision-making and judgement

The term 'Business Partner' is gaining more and more prominence within HR. It serves to remind HR professionals that their role is foremost connected to working with the business. Now, this all sounds very obvious but actually being new to your role may mean that you initially get too stuck into internal HR activities rather than have one eye on the business itself.

This is a fundamental mistake. You are not on the frontline so you need to understand how life at the coalface is lived and what goes on in the main operational roles.

In your first weeks you therefore need to ensure that you have built in time to understand how the operation works.

Back to the floor (from Lesson 5)

- Shadow people to understand not just what they do but also to find out how they feel about their role, the obstacles they face and what they would do to overcome them if they were in charge.
- If you can, try to undertake activities within some of the main roles. There is no substitute for actually stepping into someone else's shoes.
- Build in time in the coming weeks and months to revisit some of these people so you can understand recurring issues and how things have possibly moved forward for them.

Flexibility

If you understand the business well enough by this point to be able to collaborate with line managers and other employees then the next stage is all about flexibility.

Doing the right thing does not mean, although it may do sometimes, being rigid or inflexible in your approach. In my experience, HR people with little influence in the business will often hide behind their role, somebody else or another factor e.g. legal requirements. When this happens you end up 'sticking rigidly to your guns' around an issue, even if you are hearing logical opposing arguments. This can end up breeding resentment and does nothing to positively increase your impact within the company.

There will be times when you need to go against your principles or established best practice to get to a win/win solution. This isn't about being weak, it's objectively considering all angles and opinions and using a different approach because that is what is required.

An example: You may not feel it is right that someone has a disproportionate pay increase because it would be difficult to justify it to that individual's colleagues. However, the risk of losing this person could be too great for the business in terms of the person's value and so the increase may be appropriate. If you are used to talking in terms of hard facts when justifying pay increases then having to justify on the basis of someone's subjectively perceived 'value' will be new to you.

However, sometimes you may have to just swallow hard and realise that not everything can be kept in neat pigeonholes and that some decisions may appear to be less logical but can still be better for the business in the long run!

Commercial awareness

'Come down from your ivory tower – it's lunchtime!'

Commercial awareness is a popular skill nowadays and often people define it as 'knowing your business'. It's more than that though. It's about knowing what the effect on B is if you do something to A. In another way, if you spend £10 on A then that is £10 you cannot spend on B. This is about making the right choices that have the right effect on the 'bottom line' in the business.

So, you are keeping in touch with the 'floor'. However, what you are also gaining through this process is a commercial understanding of how the place runs. This is vitally important as your decisions and guidance need to have a 'commercial edge' attached. If you do not always have the business in mind then you will always be acting in isolation; in a silo that bears no resemblance to real life from others' perspectives.

Consider this example: An HR Manager in a retail superstore is asked to work with a line manager to make wage bill savings within the cashier population. The HR Manager has analysed absence and overtime and believes that the area is overstaffed by two people. The suggestion is made to the line manager that when two people leave they need not be replaced. This is commonly known as 'natural wastage'.

However, the line manager has done his own analysis of the busiest periods and impact on service.

The overstaffed hours are between 10 am and 11am and 3-4.30pm. It is therefore not as simple to say that two people should just not be replaced as this will leave the operation short before 10 am, between 11am and 3pm and again after 4.30pm! What seemed an easy solution is now a major problem! Just taking two people out is going to have serious, adverse effects that could outweigh the short term financial benefits.

Solutions to issues often have to be very creative and carefully considered. The easiest answers have often always been previously considered and discounted because they are not effective.

Commercial awareness comes into play all the time for you. Your ability to get results is directly linked to how commercially aware you are, how well you understand how the business works in detail and how you apply this with others.

Being a true partner is about making difficult commercial decisions that may land you and the manager in tribunal but were right to take to protect the business. This is where your true credibility comes into play rather than taking the soft option for your own self preservation.

How strong you are in this area is directly related to *ivory tower syndrome.* Often, those who are not in touch, not overly visible and taking decisions that are perceived to have a negative impact are said to sit in 'ivory towers'. These remote people can often work to agendas that are not in tune with how the 'masses' feel; their actions may give short term results but the impact is often felt more severely and adversely in the long run.

The trick is to make good commercial decisions that both win the battle and go some way to winning the war!

Consider the example above where the individual was given a pay rise to keep them in the business. Others could find out about this and feel it to be an unfair, short term decision that could affect the morale of others who now also want a pay increase. A way around this could be to ensure that everyone knows that the person with the pay rise now also has to achieve a certain level of target and that if others hit this target then they too will receive pay increases. A perceived unfair decision has now become more accepted because there is now a standard policy for all that everyone could benefit from, not just this one individual.

The jargon

Every business has its own cultural jargon — its own language that is unique to that business, discipline or sector. Learn it quickly.

It is very obvious to others when people have not got to grips with what it is the business does every day and your credibility will not be strengthened by having poor understanding.

Jargon can be broken into sayings, talking in acronyms or using technical words. You need to be on the same wavelength as managers/other employees and knowing the jargon can help achieve this as you also get to understand the activities within the various roles.

The industry and the market

Another way of staying in touch is to read the trade journals that are normally published weekly or monthly relating to your business.

This is an invaluable way of keeping yourself updated so you can hold your own in conversations as well as being able to clearly link new thinking and ideas to what the company requires.

Operational meetings

One of the best ways of understanding the day-to-day running of the business is to attend operational, frontline management meetings.

There may not be a need to attend every single one but you do need to develop your 'presence' to contribute where appropriate and take on board suggestions or activities that then arise. However, if you are going to attend such meetings, do make sure you have something to say and something to offer. There is nothing worse than someone taking up a valuable seat but only as a spectator!

Decision making and judgement

Decisions require justification and, above all, good judgement. Judgement is defined as 'the ability to make considered decisions or come to sensible conclusions'. It is a fantastic competency that really boosts credibility because you can be relied on for sound answers, advice and guidance.

An example:

You are getting word that there are rumblings of slight discontent from two female individuals in an otherwise successful team. They are becoming unhappy with the sexist banter that comes from their male colleagues. Their manager has told you that it's only 'a bit of fun' and that the two female employees are 'fine with things'.

You are now left with a number of considerations:

1) There is legal risk from potential costly discrimination claims (legal aspect)

2) There is a moral/welfare angle in that the two female colleagues are uncomfortable and therefore not as happy as they could be in their role/team (motivation and welfare aspect)

3) Over-reacting to events could ultimately impact on the successful team's ability to get results (commercial angle)

In this example there is a battle between duty vs commercial awareness. You have a legal duty and a moral duty to protect the business and its individuals whilst aiming to preserve the otherwise successful elements of the team. If you don't know how to achieve these objectives (i.e. you do not have the expertise) then you could decide to:

a) Ignore the situation and hope it will blow over

or

b) Focus too much on one or two of the three elements (legal, moral, commercial) at the expense of another.

Both of these options are obviously not ideal as you need to successfully deal with and balance all three considerations where possible.

Your best solution may be to take the following three fold approach:

i) Find out for yourself from the female colleagues in terms of how things are and if they have any issues – if they are generally fine but think things get out of hand now and again then:

ii) Ensure that the manager is reacting to the next bit of banter by telling the other male colleagues that they 'have gone too far' – this will help restate boundaries in the team around what is and isn't acceptable.

iii) By doing this you also have an audit trail around actions taken without the need for over formality at this stage.

The decisions you make and the guidance you give others can impact lives and also have legal and financial consequences for the business. Often, advice and decisions are taken whilst on the phone and about people you may have only even barely met!

This affords you a level of objectivity but can also potentially lead to flippancy or lazier decision making because you are less involved.

Staying on the retail theme from earlier, follow this employee relations case:

A manager phones you to say that he suspects one of his people of taking £50 out of the till. Another colleague definitely saw the person in question take the money. The manager wants your advice on how to handle this:

You have a number of options:

a) **Suspend the individual immediately**
b) **Investigate by talking to the colleague who allegedly saw the crime first and then suspend the suspect**
c) **Balance the till to understand if £50 is indeed missing.**

'Can I phone a friend?'

You may have thought that A or B were the right answers before considering C. If you had taken B as the option then this could be embarrassing if it is found that £50 is not even missing! One option not even detailed above may be to search the individual – but do you have the right to? From the beginning there are a number of considerations before you can even judge what action is required.

So let's say that £50 is indeed missing and the manager has now suspended the individual.

The suspect individual has sent in a medical certificate which covers the period in which the manager wants to hold a disciplinary interview – What do you advise?

a) **Leave it until they are fit for work**
b) **Carry out disciplinary interview anyway, even if you need to meet near the individual's home**
c) **Carry out disciplinary interview in their absence**

Again, all three seem worthwhile options. In judging what should be the best course of action, you need to consider the legal, contractual and commercial risks to each option.

If you choose A then it could be weeks before the matter is resolved and who will be covering for them in the business in the meantime? If you choose B then could this cause a legal issue if you are disregarding your duty of care to the individual? If you choose C then will this be fair and reasonable if you then dismiss and have to defend yourself in Tribunal?

All need balancing carefully – often there is no right answer and the merits of each situation need carefully weighing up.

Furthermore, someone who has been in the business for five years will need treating differently to one who has two week's service. If the same individual has become very ill then are they up to a disciplinary meeting?

Justification

As you can see, justification is important in terms of the legal framework but also to maintain harmony in the workplace so that decisions taken are not felt to be unfair. One question I always find beneficial to ask myself is:

How would I justify this in the pub?

This sounds like an odd question, but it really isn't. If you are involved in a social event, people will often ask you questions or make statements that they wouldn't necessarily say in the workplace. If drink has played a part then people are often even more forthcoming with their feelings!

So if someone says 'Why was he promoted and not me?' then you need to have a justifiable answer if you were involved in the decision or are aware of the reasons.

Similarly, if you have arranged training for one person over another then can you justify it?

This is important. It is not good enough to 'spin' your way out of situations or externalise it onto someone else (i.e. 'I was told to' or 'It was nothing to do with me' – when it was!). If you have made a decision, or played an important part in one made, then you have to be able to stand by and justify it to maintain and develop credibility.

Tell it how it is, how you or others came to the decision and admit failings if there are any. HR people are often put on a pedestal of never being allowed to make a mistake because they are the supposed upholder of standards, principles, procedures etc. But they are human and as fallible as anyone else!

So how can I improve my decision making skills (or minimise poor decision making)?

- Become an employment law expert (see **Lesson 11**) – so much of your advice will have a legal context surrounding it
- Know the business and the likely impact of your decisions on it
- Get your own mentor or someone you respect that you can lean on for your own support and guidance
- Don't be too proud to learn from your mistakes
- Try and sleep on decisions or reflect rather than giving snap answers.

Summary

- Go back to the floor initially and regularly.
- Be flexible in your approach where there is a clear, logical or factual argument present.
- Develop commercial awareness by understanding how your decisions, advice and activities affect the business.
- Don't sit in an 'ivory tower'.
- Get to know the jargon of the business and industry trends.
- Ensure you can always justify and back up your decisions.
- Revisit decisions you have made – were your judgements sound and valid?

Lesson 9

Don't be a spectator

Take and Share responsibility

'Not today, thanks – you're on your own!'

When I started out in HR I was aware of a strange contradiction at play with the other HR people around me. They would want to be seen as real business partners, working at the coalface and in the muck and bullets of the operation. However, when it came to difficult decisions those same people would utter a popular phrase,

'I can give them advice but it's up to them in terms of the management decision they then take. The accountability is theirs!'

Now, you might read this sentence and think, 'Well what's wrong with that – seems perfectly reasonable and it ensures that managers don't abdicate their responsibilities.'

Part of that is indeed correct but when I heard the phrase I would always think that what they were really saying was:

- If anything goes wrong it will be nothing to do with me!
- I'm only there for advice, nothing more!

When you break this down you can therefore see that it completely undermines the three pillars I focus on in **Lesson 1**.

These two factors give out negative messages regarding:

Expertise

What these HR people are effectively saying here is that they are so unconfident in their own level of expertise that there is an inner nervousness associated with giving advice that might backfire.

Credibility

If it's nothing to do with them when it comes to the crunch then how do they expect managers to want to be their 'partner' when HR have effectively 'done a runner'!

It's no good standing behind the old 'it's better if they take responsibility and stand on their own two feet' line.

Results

The advice and courses of action you suggest are intended to achieve the desired outcome for the manager, business etc. If you shirk your own responsibilities when things get tough then this is not going to aid getting the right result – you're the 'expert' remember.

The balance

So the overall difficulty here is about trying to strike a balance between partnering and providing expertise but not doing everything for the individual concerned. As I mention in **Lesson 6**, the idea is to try to equip and upskill managers so they are broadly self sufficient where possible. The right approach is to be less of an innocent bystander where 'it's nothing to do with me' whilst ensuring you are not a 'leave it to me, I'll do it all' type.

So let's consider an example in the employee relations field.

Brian's dismissal

Brian has allegedly stolen a laptop from the office he works in.

His manager, Simon, is carrying out a disciplinary interview and has adjourned to ring you and tell you where he is up to and give you a summary. Simon tells you that the CCTV in the office does not pick up Brian actually stealing the laptop but does show him as the last person in the office before it went missing.

The manager is asking whether there is enough evidence here to dismiss Brian fairly.

You have a number of options:

a) Tell him, "Yes there is, there is enough reasonable belief to suggest he must have done it."
b) Tell him, "No, harder evidence is required."
c) Tell him, "It's up to you," and point out the merits and drawbacks of both options.

This is a very common, real life example of the hundreds of conversations that go on between managers and HR people every day. Within the options, there are obviously other factors, e.g. the depth of your employment law knowledge and your interpretation of the word 'reasonable' in law.

The problem

If there is a lack of knowledge then this could lead to you erring on the side of caution and encouraging the manager to go for option B. This would be the safest route but, commercially, leaves you with a potential thief who could do it again and again.

It will always be easier for the HR professional to take the softest and most safest route that avoids legal claim. However, this is obviously not always going to be a great approach if then faced with the potential for further thefts as a result of your poor decision making skills or risk averse nature!

Focusing on option C is often a favourite for many HR people. They convince themselves that they are playing the role of 'objective solicitor' here but the issue for me is that HR people actually work in the business and should not have the luxury of being able to give remote take it or leave it 'advice' as opposed to giving clear instructions.

So there is a problem here that is not apparent in other functions:

In Finance, often factual advice will be given that has a clear effect on the financial situation of X if you manipulate Y.

In Marketing, previous activity or campaigns can be evaluated for their benefits, new trends and developments can be trialed.

This feels tangible. HUMAN BEHAVIOUR IS OFTEN NOT SO TANGIBLE! You cannot flick X and know the effect on Y. Unpredictable things can happen, events are not black and white and so an element of judgement is required. Often, this can be backed up by previous experience or case law in my example. However, often there are only shades of grey where human behaviour is concerned. It's often illogical and difficult to interpret.

Did Brian steal the laptop? – We may never know. It is about taking the evidence at hand and coming to a reasonable conclusion considering the needs of the business and the legal framework.

If you are just pointing out the pros and cons of the options to a manager, and nothing more, then you are putting the weight of the judgement entirely on the manager's shoulders.

You may still be thinking 'So what, it's ultimately a management decision'. Indeed it is, but only when the manager is COMFORTABLE taking the decision based on his own abilities and your expert advice, reasoning and instructions.

A doctor cannot prescribe the wrong tablets and then later claim that it was up to the individual ultimately as to whether they took them or not! The individual relied on the doctor's expertise.

Your manager relies on your expertise.

It can still be a *management decision* that the manager is happy to stand by, even under tribunal cross examination. But they have come to it partly through your guidance. It is not good enough to just give options and tell them to pick one! There has to be a preferred option in there somewhere that you BOTH then work on in terms of how sound and valid it feels so that you can BOTH then stand by it.

The solution

So far then you have three options in terms of your advice to Simon around whether or not there is enough evidence to dismiss Brian fairly.

a) Tell him, "Yes there is enough reasonable belief to suggest he must have done it."

b) Tell him, "No, harder evidence is required."

c) Tell him, "It's up to you," and point out the merits and drawbacks of both options."

In light of the above, it should not be C so you both need to come to a reasonable conclusion as to the merits of A and B.

This involves:

- Your consideration of recent case law around holding a reasonable belief that a theft has occurred. This will point to things like the thoroughness of the investigation and the procedure applied so far.

- Your understanding of the background of the individual, the background around previous losses within the business and therefore how commercially strong the argument for dismissal is.
- Whether on not the manager 'has it in' for the individual and the extent to which his judgement here may be clouded.

Get the point?

So much of this is your responsibility. So much so that it can never be something that the manager is solely accountable for if things go wrong.

You have both taken either decision A or B – you just need to be clear on a number of factors:

a) Did I provide the right factual and legal advice?

b) Did I engage the manager in the conversation so that the ultimate decision was agreed and shared?

c) Did the manager understand the potential risks and benefits associated with different actions?

d) Has the manager learned something here in the process, perhaps around the legal/procedural context or the need to be fair and objective for example?

If the above have been achieved then you have definitely upskilled the manager, perhaps more than you think you have and so similar and future conversations should be easier. You have also enforced the point of not just telling the manager the answers all the time. You have gone through the process, eliminated possible courses of action and in doing so have involved the manager in assessing the risks as well.

Critically, your credibility is intact or has even improved in the manager's eye. If it comes to appeal stage and Brian wins it, or if in the worst case scenario you end up with a failed Tribunal case then:

- this is good development for you as there will be learning
- admitting mistakes is fine if you are growing from it – managers weirdly prefer their HR people to make and admit mistakes as it makes them more 'like us'!
- your reputation should still be intact if you did not know better
- your relationship with the manager / business will still have improved or at least remained the same.

Take and share responsibility. Everybody wants a 'comrade' around them who they can lean on and share the burden with. Stay with your manager through events and don't abandon them – especially if you have the right convictions around an action taken.

Summary

- Abdicating your own responsibilities to your managers and other individuals destroys your credibility.
- Nothing is ever purely 'a management decision' where your accountabilities or responsibilities are zero.
- Human behaviour is often illogical and unpredictable – it can't all be left to a manager's judgement as there are just too many variables.
- Use your expertise to help managers decision making and to upskill them.
- You don't have to just tell manager's the answers, the responsibilities probably lie 50/50 where you are both agreeing what the answers are and the courses of action to be taken.

LESSON 10

ANALYSIS, TRENDS AND SOLUTIONS

The sexy bit!

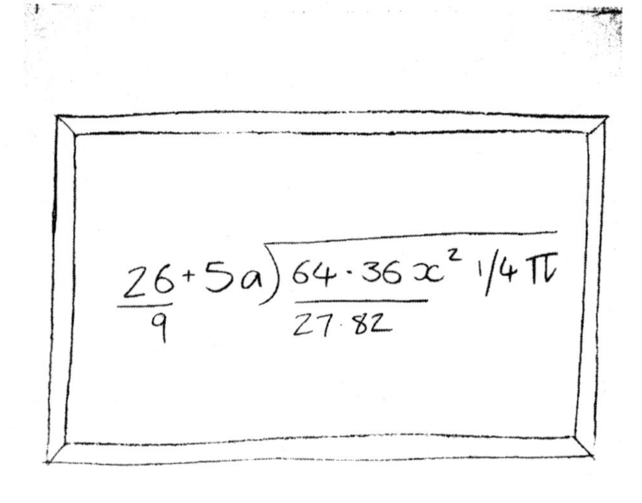

There is so much in HR today that has grown over the years but, despite attempts to cut down on administration and paperwork, the routines and reactive bits still seem to be aplenty.

You can take any job description, be it HR Advisor, Officer or Manager and there will always be various routine, often admin intensive tasks:

- Recruitment administration
- Payroll
- Employee records
- Policies and procedures
- Employee Relations activity
- Exit interviewing
- Induction

… and so on, and so on.

Depending on the level of your role, there will be varying degrees of this routine 'grunt' work but one thing is for certain: you can get so bogged down in it that your brain is not concentrating on the proactive, strategic, freeing up time, worthwhile and valuable activities that are what I call the 'sexy bits'!

Free up the routines

I remember being trained by an HR Manager years ago when I first career-changed into HR. One of the routines was to produce a two sided, A4 newsletter that was then placed in various areas in the staff restaurant.

This would have various bits of news on and the odd bit of communication. How long do you think this would take to produce, bearing in mind there was little artwork involved and it was a straightforward two page communication?

30 minutes, 1 hour perhaps?

It used to take this HR Manager half a day plus!

Now, I'm not sure if this was just 'preference over priority'. What I mean is she may have just really liked doing it and it really wasn't of critical importance to her if it took four or five hours to complete.

Of course, there were other things that needed to be done but in my time with her I observed that many hours were spent on reactive routines, rather than in any planning or link to what HR should actually be doing to move the business forward.

So before moving onto the 'sexy bits' you need to cut down the processes to the minimum.

The 80/20 rule again

In this context, the HR Manager was spending 80% of her time doing something that probably had a 20% result/impact. Most people only ever glanced at the newsletter and much of what was in it got covered in other forums, meetings etc. It is therefore safe to say that she could have spent 20% of her time on it instead, thereby making it the 20/20 rule!

This obviously isn't entirely fair and I'm exaggerating to make a point. (She didn't spend 80% of her time on it because that would have been about 35 hours!!) but the point is still valid.

What else are you doing that takes a lot of time but for very little benefit? This question itself can be challenging as some processes and procedures in your business may be well established and have never previously been challenged. You may come to the following example conclusions:

- Take up two references instead of three.
- Create two of those spreadsheets for managers, rather than three as most agree they don't look at the third one.
- Exit interviews are telling you what you already know because of the nature of the questions. Change them!

Always determine what the actual benefit is for the business. Many HR people will carry on with processes because they always have; the business likes it that way. They may also think it will affect how worthwhile HR is perceived to be if you stop doing certain things for them!

Some of the things will feel 'untouchable' but still need challenging rather than 'we have always done it because …' language.

The business instead needs to see how doing 'sexier' things will improve results even further but that it may come at the expense of things that they are used to having done for them but that have little or no real impact.

However, you need to free up your time before you can even get into 'bigger things' because, once started, these new activities often require a lot of your time and brainpower to give a real business benefit.

Let's look at two examples within a typical HR role:

Absence management example

The reactive, routine 'grunt' bit:

a) Chasing medical certificates and self certifications.

b) Entering information into a database.

c) Reactive conversations with managers when they have 'had enough of someone's absence'.

d) Writing absence policies and procedures.

e) Enforcing procedures.

f) Conversations around payments to be made (or not!).

g) Providing reports to managers around absence with the odd manager then wanting to 'really focus on this' to reduce their team absence.

h) Conversations with absent employees.

Ok, so all valuable but also all very variable in terms of the business benefit.

So, start with an objective in mind

e.g. Reduce absence from 6% to 4% in six month's time.

Great – but will you achieve this by just carrying out the activities above? Of course you won't as you are dealing with the symptoms and are getting into some of the causes but only in 'pockets'.

The 'Sexy' bit – analysis, trends and solutions

You can take some of the reactive routines to start some real analysis in this area:

1) Measure absence in the right way to give the right metric (e.g. percentage of lost time rather than just counting number of days absence).

2) What does absence cost the business in lost output?

3) Who are the Top 10 'offenders' – Can their absence be broken down into the following:

a) Short and frequent bouts – unlinked reasons – are there certain days the absence falls on?

b) Short and frequent bouts – linked reasons

c) Long term absence or hospital admission for example.

4) Is the policy then followed consistently and in order of the worst first, or just based around which manager shouts loudly enough about their team's absence?

5) Is the absence specific to a team? What are the root causes of this?

a) Is it the manager's influence?

b) Have working conditions, demands etc. changed in the team?

c) Would a team meeting or questionnaire be appropriate to understand underlying issues?

d) Does the manager require absence management training or other training around management style/skills?

6) Are you then working with the top three managers who have most issues in terms of the above activities? This would be working in 'partnership', both owning the problem and setting targets for absence reduction that you both play your part in.

7) What is now happening to the absence results? Why are you getting the successes you are getting? How is this

being communicated to other teams, the wider business etc.?

Get the idea? It's about being proactive, understanding the impact that absence has on the business and whether this impedes it from achieving its strategic objectives. For example, if a company has a strategic objective concerning customer service then a 10% absence rate will work strongly against this!

You are then using your expertise to get results, be it through training, understanding the root causes and influencing/convincing the manager with respect to the costs of absence. Done correctly, this can be a real boost to credibility as you have effectively freed up the manager's time through less stress, covering the workload etc. and they can now concentrate on more proactive activities that help them achieve other important objectives.

One more example to embed this approach:

Employee turnover example

The reactive, routine 'grunt' bit:

a) Carrying out exit interviews.

b) Providing basic statistical reporting around leaver rates in teams and why people are leaving.

c) Helping to deal with issues in teams as they arise.

d) Getting more involved in recruitment interviewing yourself to help 'get it right first time'.

Analysis, Trends and Solutions

Objective: Reduce employee turnover from 40% to 30% in six months time.

1) Identify the real reasons for leaving, not just what the exit interview tells you. For example, someone may say they are leaving for more money but actually they were underperforming. Did they leave because they couldn't/didn't want to do job or was it partly the manager's fault?

2) Why do some managers have higher turnover of employees than others?

3) Are people leaving within a certain length of service timeframe – does this point to quality of induction, for example?

4) What three things has the manager committed to do differently to help reduce their turnover? It is easier to continually justify why people leave a team but at some point something has to demonstrably change.

5) Does the manager understand the financial impact of turnover on their business?

6) Is the issue in the recruitment process, induction, training, management style, pay etc.?

Again, partner with the managers of the teams with the worst figures and actively stick with them over time so that you are both working towards and then share the success of any reductions in turnover.

This is all not as easy as it sounds. You will find that you run out of ideas, your creativity dries up, you have over analysed to the point where you are unsure where to go next. This is common. Like weight loss, an individual can get so far and then it becomes harder to see further benefits!

Often, the business may then need to take riskier or more radical, expensive measures to address the situation. E.g. pay rates may be the overarching issue.

It's again about knowing when to make these sorts of recommendations. Commercially, you can't just default to these 'quick fix' solutions in the short term as they are often impractical, expensive or lack the background research. Like anything, you need to try and 'do more with less'; if you can achieve results with your managers with as 'little' as possible then your own standing, worth and credibility is improved in turn.

Summary

- Challenge the reactive, routine, normally administrative processes and procedures in your function.
- Free up time so that you can focus on analysis, identifying trends and recommending/implementing solutions.
- Think 80/20 rule – what is the input workload versus the degree of business benefit?
- Agree objectives with teams and then get into the pro-active plans and activities that will help achieve them.
- Don't abandon the manager – focus on the key people and stay with them until the end.
- Ask of managers and teams 'what do you need to do differently to achieve this objective'.
- Know when you have gone as far as you can and when more radical, riskier, expensive options may need to be considered by the business heads.

LESSON 11
LOVE EMPLOYMENT LAW!

One of the most interesting, ever changing and complex activities in a generalist HR role is to deal with and advise on employment law to managers and employees.

I have pulled this subject out, above others, because it is often the one that line managers particularly are most fearful of. They often need a lot of support with it and the business is rightly fearful of costly errors in terms of how it deals with its people.

It is also one of the most tangible activities with which an HR professional can really demonstrate their value and worth. Delivered correctly, it can save the business tens of thousands of pounds in legal costs, claims and administration.

However, this is an area that too many HR people shy away from because:

- Some people find it to be a dry subject and difficult to grasp.
- It changes constantly.
- There is a lack of confidence around what can be a complicated subject.
- There is a perception that HR can't be an expert at it and inevitably a solicitor will be required anyway.
- They believe that only a working knowledge is required in an HR role.

This is a shame.

Employment law has never been more important and has developed massively over the last three decades. The legal landscape is changing all the time and it is virtually impossible and rare that any of your line managers will keep up to date enough to never require specialist advice.

It is an area that you can show real expertise in and great advice, backed up by hard legal fact, can set you apart from your peers in HR and give your credibility a real boost.

Much of your knowledge can come from the many employment law textbooks available aimed not only at the legal profession but at HR professionals also.

It is critically important, however, to gain more than just a working knowledge. A great HR generalist can provide sound day-to-day advice without referral to others for the answers. One of the things I always found useful in the beginning was to tell someone that I was considering their legal question or issue and would come back to them. I would then go away and delve into the textbooks or research via the internet for a sound answer!

It is all important to keep yourself updated and this alone can't be underestimated. Knowing the regulations is one thing but Employment Tribunals and the bodies above them are always setting new 'precedents' to follow. This can mean that your understanding of the law one week can be very different to how it should then be applied the following week!

The main trade journals have a weekly legal column that should always be read and understood:

- Personnel Today
- People Management (CIPD)

Both journals are invaluable in this area but there are now also hundreds of websites performing the same role.

Find your sources, stick to them and make it a regular routine to understand how the law has changed or developed on a regular basis. When reading a case summary, try and guess the outcome in terms of how the tribunal/courts interpreted matters.

Of course, there will always be times when professional legal advice has to be taken. The higher risk the issue, the more likely it is that you will require professional support. Your challenge, though, is to try and keep this to a minimal level and to seek reassurance as little as possible.

This does not mean that you should arrogantly push forward with only half the answer or an unconfident one. Mistakes, as I have said, can be costly and at the end of the day you are not a qualified legal professional.

But employment law has become a pivotal role within the generalist HR role and employees increasingly expect HR to have the answers in this area. So be an expert, keep updated, attend any legal briefings run by professional firms and set yourself up as a mini lawyer for your business.

In terms of other skills, the learning of employment law and understanding how case law has developed can help develop your own judgement and ability to interpret issues and come up with good solutions. (See **Lesson 8).**

You see, it forces you to look dispassionately and objectively at issues rather than getting caught up in others' 'tabloid' ways of looking at things that can often cloud your own judgement.

You may alternatively find yourself within a business where your employment law knowledge is not really required, i.e. there is an in-house lawyer or separate advisors are used. Do not let this stop you from getting to know this all important subject. Employment law is one of those things that is mastered over years because of the many hundreds of cases, judgements and interpretations. Get the exposure now or face being potentially left behind later on.

Employment law textbooks, as I'm sure you are aware, are particularly hefty and cumbersome. There are, however, some key subjects that you need to generally have a good working knowledge of, because of their relevance to business or as a result of current developments within that area of law.

Contracts of employment and variation

Employment law begins with the nature of the contract of employment, how it is constructed and how you can vary it. It's one of the most important subject areas because everyone in employment has one.

Issues with contracts normally arise because you are looking to rely on a term within one that an employee may not be happy with (e.g. a mobility clause), or because you want to vary the contract and may need the employee's permission (e.g. you may want to widen post termination restrictive covenants).

Discipline, grievance and dismissal

Always a major topic for many businesses, you need to know the law in this area like the back of your hand, particularly as procedural elements have become even more important in recent years.

There is also a link here to **Lesson 16** as two of the five fair reasons for dismissal: conduct and capability, are so relevant in managing underperformance situations. Much of the case law in this area often surrounds interpretation of the word 'reasonable' and so this is not as black and white as you may think.

Redundancy

Similarly, redundancy is as topical as ever and at some point you will be handling the process from original announcement right up to tribunal stage in the worst case scenarios. Your business will have its own redundancy policy/terms but there are associated skills in this area needed around employee welfare, support and outplacement programmes for example.

Discrimination/Equal Opportunities

Discrimination law continues to evolve and can be extremely costly for businesses, particularly as it requires no qualifying service around an individual's right to bring a legal claim.

Many organisations are tightening up and developing equal opportunities policies, partly to act as a responsible employer but also as part of their employer branding strategy to attract and retain people.

Complaints around discrimination can be very difficult to manage and need to be handled sensitively. HR play a key part in this as they can often act as the conduit and help resolve issues and avoid tribunal at an early stage.

Family friendly regulations

The last ten years has seen an explosion in flexible working policies and the whole concept of 'family friendly working'. It is part of the work/life balance influence and partly designed to reduce the stresses and strains on working parents so that they do not have to compromise work against domestic demands.

The right to request flexible working is a key part of law here that you will be involved with at some stage and, not for the first time, you will need to help the business balance its needs against the nature of an employee's request.

Duties of ex-employees

Depending on the type of business you work for, this will be more or less important. Many contracts of employment include post termination covenants that restrict individuals in terms of where they may work or how they can develop their business. This is particularly so in sales businesses where an individual may have developed a client portfolio that the company wants to protect when the employee leaves.

In the worst cases you may be involved in injunctions or legal proceedings to hold an ex employee to their various obligations.

TUPE

This legislation is concerned with protecting employee's rights when a business is taken over by another. Obviously, a new owner may want to substitute with their own people but the law prevents them from being able to do this.

It may only come your way once or twice in your career and is often best learned and 'read up on' when, generally, your business is faced with a change of ownership or is looking to acquire another business.

Trade Union law

Again, this will only affect you if you recognise a Trade Union within your business, although discipline rules allow for any employee to be accompanied to formal meetings by a Trade Union representative.

Role of Employment Tribunals

Hopefully, you may never need to go to one or receive a claim that requires a response. I would advise, however, that you have a working knowledge of how the Tribunal system works so that you are not in a state of panic if facing one for the first time!

The system is not as formal as you may think and often things are dealt with on a common sense basis. Try to attend one as an observer if you can as this can give you a different perspective when advising line managers, especially if you can articulate to them the consequences of getting things wrong!

Provisions of various Employment Acts

Finally, as new Employment Acts come into existence, so you need to know the provisions of them and the various regulations. Many solicitors offer legal briefings to help keep you up-to-date with new regulations and their own early interpretation of them. New laws generally come into force in April and October of each year so it is easier to understand developments in employment law.

Summary

- Don't shy away from employment law as an area of your role.
- Become an expert in employment law for your business.
- Keep yourself regularly updated.
- Use the interpretation of employment law and how different cases have been handled as a way to develop your own judgement skills.

Lesson 12
Appraisals Don't Work!

'So how do you think you have done this year?'
'Amazingly well. So, what pay rise am I in line for?'

In the introduction to this book I stated that I would not be getting into too much best practice detail when it comes to HR activity, instead the focus is on how you get to grips with HR as a profession and get results through your activities.

However, I make no apology by devoting a whole lesson to: *The Dreaded Appraisal.*

Why? Well, the appraisal as an activity in business is often the single most difficult thing for managers to effectively grasp and for employees to warm to and engage with. It is often a cumbersome paper process that is often mocked and humoured (ever seen 'The Office' on the BBC?) and most people will run to the hills when they hear the word! It's most definitely a swearword to some!

The thing is, appraisal can accomplish many things in one tidy meeting and the following are all required in a great performance management system:

- Opportunity for structured discussion and feedback between manager and individual
- Identifying training and development needs
- Possible link to pay rises
- Review of performance
- Setting new goals and objectives

However, the process often feels:

- Time consuming
- Steeped in 'HR' paperwork
- There are too many processes/activities within it

- Challenging and emotional if pay or career progression is linked to this one conversation
- Like a chore for managers who then put off doing them
- To the individual that this is a very formal document that sits forever on the personnel file
- That it suffers from 'recency' where the individual feels that the manager is only reviewing them based on recent events, rather than a year's performance.

Also, if people want to discuss issues, concerns or performance with their manager then shouldn't it be encouraged that they do this as needed rather than waiting for a formal, overly paper driven review? Some managers could use paperwork and some wouldn't, depending on how appropriate it was to the conversation. E.g. if a manager was dealing with underperformance then they would be documenting their concerns, confirming new targets/objectives etc. A more informal conversation about how to improve performance further may not have any paperwork at all. It's about what feels right for the manager and individual jointly; they are both adults and surely this shouldn't be a parent/child thing?

So why do businesses continue with appraisals?

Probably because everyone else does! They have been around for so long and are so embedded into businesses that it requires a great leap of faith to even consider doing away with them.

The problem with scrapping traditional appraisal systems is that HR and senior management have a fear that if there is not a rigid process in place then certain things just won't happen e.g.:

- Performance conversations
- Training needs analysis
- Fair pay reviews based on performance review
- Succession planning
- 'How are you' one to ones between manager and individual
- The caring, motivational bit.

But isn't it even worse to force an annual process where two people are thrown together to achieve all of these things in under two hours if possible?

Often, managers cannot spare the time that the annual appraisal demands and so put it off or rush through it to fill in the paper and the process is empty. This leads to HR policing it and badgering managers to complete the process so that HR can get a 100% completion rate – effectively to 'tick the boxes'.

Adopting a more flexible approach removes the 'forced' nature that a rigid annual appraisal system can have. You can also see by now that an alternative philosophy could help the credibility of HR as the faceless, paper driven image of it is removed. It also encourages you to support and upskill managers on a day-to-day, 52 weeks a year basis when it comes to motivating and developing their staff.

This is distinctly different to tying up lots of time in annual appraisal training that can focus managers too much on process rather than the substance of what they should be trying to achieve in reality with their people on a daily basis.

What often happens is that the process gets reviewed by HR/managers every so often and a new paper process is then drawn up. It's intended to be easier and simpler to use but still has the awful hallmarks of formality and rigidity surrounding it.

The other reason that businesses do not deviate away from a stereotypical annual appraisal process is that often there is a good percentage of managers and individuals who really buy in and get a lot out of it. If you are in a business where this is a reality then you are one of the lucky ones. More often than not this will not be the case! Any changes to the process to make things 'simpler' will often be resisted by the compliant managers who argue that the process is being diluted or dumbed down in favour of other managers who can't be bothered. They will argue, quite rightly, that the paperwork should not be simplified and that instead managers should be trained to complete it correctly and in a timely way or that the company should find better managers!

So why doesn't HR spearhead scrapping it?

My view here is that HR like traditional annual appraisals as they give control, put things into neat pigeonholes and apparently make things less time consuming.

For example, if HR wants to understand the average skill levels in the business it simply adds up the gradings from all appraisals. HR tells itself that this is a great bit of analysis to be able to make other things happen. However, the gradings may be subjective or other agendas may have been at play when the manager was scoring! Gradings and ratings can also be counter-productive as everyone would probably consider themselves to be 'A Player' so you can potentially face an uphill battle trying to convince someone that they are graded 'C'.

Also, if a manager can get all the performance comments down on a neat form then that saves having to hold other review meetings throughout the year, doesn't it?!

You see, appraisals just seem to be there to make life easier for everyone apart from the individual who apparently it is designed for! When did anyone ever say 'I can't wait for my appraisal'?

So what are the alternatives to the traditional annual appraisal system?

In the introduction I highlighted the sorts of objectives that an appraisal system needs to achieve. In one of the businesses I worked for, we had a traditional annual appraisal but it was there as an option only for those managers and individuals who were familiar and comfortable with using it. So how are the other areas, normally within an appraisal process, otherwise dealt with?

Performance reviews

HR is instrumental in supporting and upskilling managers so that they are able to hold meaningful and regular one to ones with staff that let them know where they stand. This is about recognising good performance, confronting underperformance and motivating individuals towards better performance.

As long as managers are having regular, timely conversations and documenting as appropriate in this area then this is more than adequate.

'Nipping issues in the bud' is always going to be a more productive approach rather than waiting for an artificial point of the year to sort things out.

Training and Development

In most of the businesses I have worked in, I make sure that all our courses, materials, workshops etc. are detailed extensively on the company intranet. That way everyone knows what is available to them all year round, rather than waiting for the appraisal meeting to find out what the manager was going to 'suggest' for them.

This encourages people to be in charge of their own development rather than expecting the manager to always have all the answers.

Succession Planning

Here, HR is again instrumental. Rather than just capturing information from bits of paper, HR should be having proactive, meaningful and rolling all year round conversations with managers about future requirements in teams. This encourages managers to partner with HR and analyse what is needed and who should be working towards which roles. It also has more value to the employee as the manager/employee will be meeting and discussing career development when the timing is right for both parties.

Pay Reviews

I prefer to stop linking these to appraisals because they rely heavily on the subjective approach of the manager and whether they 'like' the person. Any ratings given also have a large degree of subjectivity attached to them. Instead, you can make more use of market rate information and then place it in bandings linked to factual key performance indicators (e.g. individual sales achieved across the year). I'm not saying this is a perfect system but I have yet to come across any system that is foolproof in ensuring that everyone gets exactly the right salary due to them!

First steps to change things for good

You have to look at what works best (or isn't working) for the majority. If the defenders of the appraisal system are few then you need to understand what will appeal to the masses without compromising the objectives of appraisal itself.

You can do this in the following ways:

- Understand from a cross section of managers and individuals what works well and not so well for them in the current process
- How the system could be improved – be radical!
- How you can get universal buy in
- Trial any new system to understand its impact
- Review your trial before any main roll out

You may be reading this thinking – 'How can I possibly influence this in my first HR role'? Well, you probably can't but at least you can start to appreciate the issues within traditional appraisal systems and always be sure that you are focusing on what both parties are getting out of the process rather than just completing paperwork to 'tick the box'.

Summary

- The traditional appraisal system often does not work and generally has a bad name in businesses.
- It's about individuals and for individuals so consider what they would benefit most from, not just what HR or senior management would like!
- Don't just change or simplify the paperwork – take a more radical approach.
- Trial any new system in one or two teams.

LESSON 13
RECRUITMENT WITH A 'TWIST'
Peeling back the layers

A key part of the HR role is concerned with recruitment activity and a major part of this is the skill of interviewing others. Line managers will feel it to be a good idea to get HR's involvement or it will come as a standard part of your role that someone at some point thought was relevant and important to include.

But why?

Is it because HR is a 'people' activity, recruitment is a 'people' activity so it makes sense to put the two together?

Is it because it's highly administrative so HR can do the associated paperwork attached to the process?

Perhaps it's because there should be a real point, worth and value to HR being involved?

Ah, now lets rest on that third one for a bit then.

Why are you involved in the interview process?

This is not as simple a question as it sounds. Many organisations will want you to perhaps first or second interview people or get involved with the design and delivery of assessment centres or other activities. The problem is that it's usually felt to be a good idea for HR to be involved without really considering why and what they bring to the party.

If the basic premise is that HR has more expertise then before we look at what levels/roles they should indeed be interviewing for let's first consider this expertise point.

Recruitment expertise – competencies

Many years ago, in an effort to try and replicate great people within businesses, organisations tried to establish what 'good' looked like. This involved interviewing successful employees and observing what the personal characteristics were that contributed to their success. Then, each indicator could be broken into crude knowledge, skill and attitude strands.

As this developed and HR people got hold of the process so 'competencies' were identified. A competency can be defined as an ability, knowledge or skill to do something successfully. Subsequently, the indicators could then be grouped into easy, manageable competencies that you could then attract, select, train or even pay against.

E.g. the 'planning and organising' competency could have the following indicators:

- Writes daily 'to do' lists
- Sets rolling medium term objectives for themselves
- Prioritises their work effectively
- Builds in time to allow for setbacks – contingency planning and so on.

Sounds easy, but then it got a bit complicated!

Going a step further, it was evident that completing a 'to do' list was surely not one of the predominant indicators of what 'good' would look like in a high risk, high accountability director level role! Of course not. That's why competency levels were then developed.

E.g. planning and organising

Level 1 – Individual writes 'to do' lists, prioritises work effectively

Level 2 – Individual plans and sets objectives for the medium term, builds in time for setbacks – contingency planning

Level 3 – Individual has a longer term, more strategic plan, keeps to the plan despite setbacks.

Get the idea?

This all looks very cosy and indeed gives a framework for a number of businesses to work well within. It has also, however, become cumbersome with some companies having anywhere from 10 to 15 competencies, each with up to 7 levels in each. That could be anything up to 100 indicators plus!

Subsequently, HR people have then got involved in recruitment at the point of the 'structured CBI (Competency Based Interview)'.

This will involve asking normally pre-prepared questions relating to the competency and level which in turn relate to the type of role being recruited. Often, grade scorings will be attributed to each competency so that you can then arrive at a total average score for the CBI.

It's all quite precise and technical, isn't it? Well, that's why HR has been deemed to be so worthwhile here. As the 'experts', they are better placed to apparently interpret the answers to CBI questions and give robust scorings. This all sounds quite straightforward and correct but, as you will see, the reality is often quite different.

The first issue – an admin task!

Basically, it's all got so complicated and paper driven, what with up to 100 indicators to think about every time you do an interview, that the process then often looks like this:

1) A first interview may be a structured CBI with HR

2) The second interview may be the 'main one' with the line manager who asks the 'tough' questions and really gets under the skin of how capable the candidate is, now that the compulsory CBI bit is out of the way!

See the problem? CBI has become another HR obstacle to be 'gotten over'. Managers just want to get on and recruit someone but are aware that they themselves or HR need to carry out a CBI and then the grades will need to be taken into account before offering someone a job. It becomes a bit like psychometric tests. The test may show someone as unsuitable but the manager likes them so takes them on anyway! It's the same here potentially. The CBI outcome isn't great but the manager likes them so will recruit them anyway. HR's involvement has been near pointless!

The second issue – you need to be psychic!

If you or the manager is carrying out a CBI then this will involve asking the question, capturing the answer or evidence on paper and moving on to the next question. Often, particularly in assessment centres, the interpretation and scoring is carried out later on when there is more time! This is a ridiculous false economy. If you only have the captured answers to set questions on your pad then that is all you have to go on later. If you then aren't sure about their planning and organising ability, for example, then you can't go back and ask the candidate as they have since left! You then have to score or make an assessment based on what you have in front of you or what you think the person is probably like in this skill area. This is all very random! I have seen many interviewers come out of CBIs and say things like – 'I *think* they are a 2 in this area as they are *probably* not good at…'

It's worth saying that this isn't always the case and where the CBI works well it is where HR is truly using its expertise and 'peeling back the layers' during the interview, rather than just asking basic questions, writing the answers down, giving a subjective score and moving to the next question.

The solutions

HR should be involved because they uniquely understand **BEHAVIOUR,** have an in depth understanding of competencies and can take someone's answers and then ask supplementary questions that 'peel back the layers' to get to the heart of how strong someone really is in relation to a competency.

Too often, the process is robotic. As I have said, the interviewer asks the question, writes down the answer and then moves on to a completely different question and so on. For example, take the following example question that tests planning and organising skills:

Q Give me an example of a time you successfully organised an event?

A I had to plan a party for 20 people at work which went very well and everyone said it went well.

You could stop there, score it appropriately (probably quite highly on the basis of this one answer) or you can continue on...

Q What would you have done differently in relation to planning and organising next time around?

A Well, I would have probably allowed more time in planning for the music as it was late notice for the band so I had to get another one at the last minute.

Q Why didn't you allow time in your plan for unexpected events?

A Because things are normally ok and I don't generally need it.

Now, does that change your scoring, interpretation, and reduce the need for you to have to be 'psychic' after the interview? It probably does as now we observe an individual who isn't quite all that when it comes to planning and organising and tends to go 'to the wire' on some things.

You can only carry out this layered questioning if you have really got into what planning and organising as a behaviour is about. You need to relate it to what this person will face in the role and therefore challenge heavily the printed CBI questions in front of you that may not even be that relevant. Eg. is the above question around planning an event relevant to ask a Financial Director who has a PA?!

If you are seen as a point of behavioural expertise then you probably do not need to be involved in every role being recruited for in the business. Your expertise is needed for the higher risk, higher accountability roles. Interviewing everyone at every level just dilutes WHY you are doing it – it's not just about someone having to get the admin heavy CBI out of the way, it's about bringing you in because **behavioural expertise** is uniquely required. This may therefore just apply to management roles, or the higher grades.

Finally, I mentioned before that often the line manager 'real life' interview is often seen as the most valuable.

However, in reality it often isn't the case because a line manager may ask a very narrow set of questions because they are looking for someone 'like themselves'.

They may only be satisfied when they are confident that they can work with that person. The interviewee's skill, knowledge, talent etc. may have relatively little to do with it!

HR can therefore strengthen its part by carrying out a highly concentrated version of CBI where they focus in on no more than three key behaviours (that 'power of three' again!) that are needed for the role/team and then begin to peel back the multiple layers to the point of interrogation!

This should then allow you to give feedback to the candidate as you go along and during the interview so that you can get a reaction and have more of a conversation. Done correctly, it even becomes a bit of a 'life coach' or 'career counselling' situation that can really illuminate the real behaviours (rather than the artificial 'interview behaviours') of the individual and give you a greater sense of their character and likely effectiveness.

Where this has worked well for me, I have even noticed that it buys the candidate into the business even more as it is not a straightforward Q and A session and, consequently, the individual believes that your analysis of them is a sign that the company cares about the motivations of its people.

E.g.

- 'Would it be fair to say that you are confused about what you are really looking for in your next role?'
- 'It sounds like you have identified three things here, which of these three would really make the difference for you?'
- 'It seems to me that the theme in everything you are saying is more about making money for yourself rather than developing a team around you?'

It's about analysing a candidate's answers and stating your own judgements or offering your own opinions to either 'push buttons' or get the candidate to reflect on something they perhaps hadn't before. This gives a much greater sense of the individual's potential faring against the competencies or behaviours you are looking for.

This kind of feedback, played back to the line manager, then becomes invaluable and you become an invaluable part of the process rather than a robotic, pre-prepared and structured questioner! You know you're getting somewhere if the manager has decided they like or don't like a candidate but your credible feedback has forced them into a rethink!

Summary

- Consider whether your expertise should be involved in recruiting EVERY role in the business/unit.
- Understand competencies to an in-depth level, which ones are vital to a role and to what degree.
- Minimise the competencies and number of prescribed, structured questions used in a CBI interview.
- Steer away from just asking the pre-set questions, recording answers and moving swiftly to the next one!
- Focus on supplementary questions that 'peel back the layers' to understand the candidates day-to-day, real behaviours.
- Feedback to the candidate and state your own opinions of them during the interview as appropriate to further test and challenge them.

LESSON 14
ABANDON BORING TRAINING

'David Smith – The best trainer in town!'

At some point in your role you will be involved in the design and delivery of training, be it in 121 format, a coaching style or as a classroom workshop. I am going to focus on the latter here for a number of reasons:

- It is the format that is widely used in a stereotypical way, full of the normal training clichés and associated activities.

- It's often the format that is hardest to get right because of the different needs and make up of the audience.
- Classroom training can often run from half a day to a few days and so needs to be able to hold the attention of its audience and make them want to come back for more!

Design and delivery

There are hundreds of training books on the market that will look to point you in the right direction when it comes to the most effective way of getting your message across. It would be very easy to replicate that here but, instead, I want to de bunk some of the apparently 'tried and tested' methods that I simply don't believe work all that well. Why? Because it's a bit like my review of the validity of appraisals in **Lesson 12**. You see, appraisal systems will always work well for the minority who buy into it, love the paperwork and look forward to them.

Training workshops are the same. The usual design and delivery style really only appeals to a certain section of the audience. Like teaching in a school, you need various 'weapons' and 'hooks' so that everyone buys in at some point throughout the session.

So what do I mean by 'stereotypical' design and delivery?

PowerPoint

The phrase 'Death by PowerPoint' has become fashionable in recent years. No wonder! People use it as a 'crutch', as a script so that individual style, flair or creativity is not required. Just read off the screen and away you go. My major issue with this is that not only is it boring but:

- There is too much on the screen – a 6/6 rule is preferable where you may have 6 points with no more than 6 words for each point
- It becomes monotonous as the trainer reads the PowerPoint along with the trainee reading it too. This is a bit like 'Janet and John' and as if you are teaching someone how to read!
- No one is really listening as they have moved on to read the rest of the PowerPoint slide and so are not taking in what you are even teaching them anyway.

It's all just very lazy. Stand up training instead needs to be a 'performance'. You need to have honed your script beforehand in your head. To that end...

Your Introduction ...

... Or should I say the dreaded 'Icebreaker bit' – I am convinced that these are only used entirely for the trainer's benefit to relieve any awkward opening training moments when all eyes are on them.

Icebreakers outside of just introducing who the trainees are, where they are from etc. are absolutely pointless and a little bit cringe-worthy. It is completely unnatural to interview the person next to you and then tell the rest of the group their claim to fame or what animal they would like to be! It adds nothing, it doesn't really break any ice (assuming that there is indeed ice that needs breaking) and is nothing to do with what the main body of the training is about. It invariably leads to an awkward pause, a kind of 'now that's out of the way let's get on with the training' moment.

'Hooks'

Your training needs 'hooks' – it needs stand out moments that people sit up and listen to, be it :

- A shocking story or fact
- Great use of humour
- An activity that no one was expecting

'Hooks' are also about 'peeks behind the curtain'. If you are about to have a break in the training, let the audience know what is coming up and leave them on a 'cliffhanger'. It's only what good TV does to hold someone's attention.

'Turn it on its head' moments

These are the unexpected parts of the session that make people sit up and realise that this isn't just another run of the mill session and that it's actually going to be quite fun and may even hold their attention ... even into the post lunch 'graveyard shift'!

Example

- Tell them at the beginning that you're not interested in icebreakers and instead that you're going to get straight on with why you are all there.

- Introduce different coloured toys and 'playthings' that can be thrown around the room, left on the table for use etc. It's just something unexpected that lets people know that this is a little bit different.

- Acknowledge openly that there are people in the session who just don't want to be there, have been sent by the manager and are basically 'hostages'. Tell them your mission is for them to leave here knowing more than when they arrived. Use this as a bit of a 'clapometer' where you then check at various points as to whether the 'hostages' are any happier. It's a good way of defusing tension and again gets away from the 'trainer as teacher' image.

Role plays

This is where people are forced to 'act unnaturally' in front of others, usually in ridiculous artificial situations just so the trainer and the rest of the audience can act as 'X Factor' style judges and give 'feedback'.

No one likes them and some people feel physically sick at the prospect of having to take part in one! The trainer tells the audience that the role play is only a reflection on a real life situation but it just isn't.

I'm not sure I can really think of a situation where someone has actually then put into practice something that has come out of a role play. However, the intention is valid. Trainees should work on their own in small groups but without others staring at them and judging them. With the right evaluation afterwards, this is more effective and ultimately achieves the same objectives.

Lots of handouts ...

...will just go in the bin or get left behind in a lot of cases. One delegate pack is enough and should contain only what is absolutely vital for trainees to refer to post training.

Flipcharts

Another pet hate. It normally goes like this:

'How do you think a customer feels when they have had bad service'

The trainer then writes up the words that the audience has come up with.

'Angry'

'Feeling like they won't come back'

'Humiliated'

'Feel like a number'

OK. So what is the point?

Rather patronisingly, these words will then have to be written down by the group or, worse, will be available in their handout pack! But again, WHAT'S THE POINT? The trainees are not going to go back to work thinking about these words as if they have discovered for the first time that someone getting bad customer service is going to feel 'angry'!

Even worse still is the trainer who writes these words up on a flipchart and then turns the page almost as soon as the last bit is written to then concentrate on the next subject!

Training Duration

Whenever I see an advert for a two day workshop I always take 50% off because that is what the length should probably be. However, to justify the cost or the trainers time or as a result of some other agenda, training always seems to get padded out!

Once you have built in pointless icebreakers, overlong exercises and the wading through of hefty workbooks you can see why the training session now runs across five days.

People learn in short bursts and training is most effective if it lasts about 90 minutes or so. This may mean that it's 90 minutes a day for five days. This forces the trainer to be getting the vital things into the session that are going to hit the mark first time. Obviously, short bursts over different days can often be quite difficult to accommodate, which is why the lazy trainer may look to spread a one day session out with lots of exercises etc. to keep reinforcing the points already made.

If the training is slick and well thought through then it can, however, be delivered in a much shorter timeframe.

It may be that post training 'catch ups' should be built in or that the training is carried out once a month. This is better in terms of trainees retaining information but, sadly, trainers will want to get things out of the way in one go rather than having to come back weekly or monthly in a more fragmented way which takes more planning (but is probably more effective in the long run)!

Hopefully, you can see where I am going with all of this. The trainer is often just forgetting the whole point of why the trainee is there. The trainee needs to LEARN and RETAIN information, skills etc. Everything you do as a trainer needs to align to this, not just rattle through things on auto pilot without really thinking just to say that individuals have been 'trained' and you can tick that off the 'to do' list.

Let's take two examples, one around what I call stereotypical training and the other a better example that encourages learning and retention of information.

Customer service scenario

The trainees work in a department store and are coming to you to improve their customer service skills.

There are eight people in the group and you are aware that time is limited because there is minimal cover provided when they are away from the 'shop floor'.

Example One: Customer service training workshop

9.00 Tea

9.15 Introductions and Icebreaker:

"What is your greatest fear?"

"What is your claim to fame?"

"What animal would you be?"

9.45 "Why are we here?" – Aims and objectives of session (flipchart), "What do you want to get out of today?" (flipchart)

10.00 "What is customer service?" (Group discussion and flipchart – refer to workbook and write answers)

10.15 "What chain stores do we admire in terms of good customer service?" "Why have we chosen these?" (Group discussion and flipchart – refer to workbook and write answers)

10.35 Break

10.50 Role play – four groups of two – one person is the sales assistant and one is the customer. Rest of group to give feedback.

Each group should give an example of bad service and then good service. Feel free to make up your own scenario.

Rest of audience to write what they observe in their workbooks and the learning points from the good service role plays.

Five minutes prep time, ten minutes for each group to role play their two scenarios.

11.45 "What conclusions did we come to?" (write in workbook)

12.00 "What are the costs of bad service?" – Flipchart example of a disgruntled customer telling nine other people about their bad experience – "What effect would this have on profits?" (Discussion, write answers in workbook)

12.30 Lunch

OK, lets stop there for now. It's safe to say that this session will probably go on all day and just continuously reinforce the need for good customer service.

Has it changed behaviour in its trainees though?

Example Two: Customer service training workshop

9.00 Introduction, why we are here, stress that we are going to get 'under the skin' of customer service today and why it's just not as good as it should or could be.

9.15 Environment: 'We know what good customer service looks like so why aren't we doing it?' (Group discussion, list key points raised on one side of flipchart)

9.25 "Lets take each point in turn and look at the barriers and what you need to overcome them."

E.g.: Always thinking about stock that needs to be put out, no time to spend with the customer.

Solution? Better shift planning so that replenishment can be carried on out of hours.

10.00 Attitude: 'Do you want to give good customer service?' "What do you honestly think about customers'?"

Group discussion regarding attitudes, each individual needs to write down any negatives they associate with customer service and how they could personally overcome them, if at all.

10.30 Break

10.45 Show group video of one of their colleagues who had agreed to be filmed giving bad customer service in a real life example.

"How would you feel if you were that customer?"

'How has this taped recording changed how you will approach service going forwards?'

Group Discussion

11.15 Action Plan – What three things will you be doing differently beyond today?

Trainers Action Plan – The top three concerns you have about your environment will go back to your manager who will then feed back on changes that can be made to help you give better service.

We will meet again in one month for one hour to review the progress you have made with your action points...

Close at 11.30am

See how different this is? The video is unexpected, turns things on its head. The fact that the trainer is going to help out in the workplace issues is different again. It recognises that there is no point in the trainees changing their attitude and behaviours if the environment is poor. It shows that the trainer genuinely wants to help change the approach to customer service. Trainees are only encouraged to write down the things that they will need to rely on when putting their action plans into effect.

Example One is a very dry, very formula driven training session and will probably have little impact in terms of changing behaviour. It also gets to lunchtime without achieving much whilst *Example Two* has achieved a great deal by 11.30am!

Evaluation

I have built this into the second example and it's vitally important – the all important topic that is on everyone's lips in the training arena and demonstrates the impact that learning has had on business results.

When the trainees return in one month, the progress with action plans can be measured and the tangible impacts on customer service can then be assessed. It would be very difficult to evaluate later on when it comes to *Example One* as the trainees are virtually left with nothing to actually go away and do post workshop.

Concentrating on what happens after workshops is of paramount importance. As I have said, training for training's sake does nothing to commit learned knowledge to long term memory or help develop a skill for the longer term. A tip is to focus on this post workshop activity and how you will demonstrate the impact of training before you actually get into writing training content. Too often, evaluation is left as an after thought as the last thing to quickly do ahead of rolling training out. Spending a disproportionate time on evaluation in your planning will reap greater benefits in terms of results down the line.

Always remember, training and development is not about people just ticking boxes. Only when changed behaviour is actually evident in an individual or where a new skill is then actively being used can it be said that someone has DEVELOPED. The whole thing should be difficult; take people out of their comfort zones, force them to make and learn from mistakes because that's ultimately how people learn. It's surely the same as being in a Gordon Ramsey kitchen as a trainee chef!

Summary

- There are a lot of stereotypical training formats used that potentially achieve little and result in an aversion to wanting to attend training workshops.
- Your training needs an element of the unexpected to gain attention and hold interest; this promotes effective learning.

- Training, where possible, should be given in short bursts with follow up activity to reinforce the learning.
- From the beginning, think about how you will evaluate the impact of your training on the business. Does the format and activities within the workshop make evaluation easy?
- Spend longer than you would on the evaluation part of your training design / plan.

Lesson 15
DEVELOPING MANAGERS
What's in your toolbox?

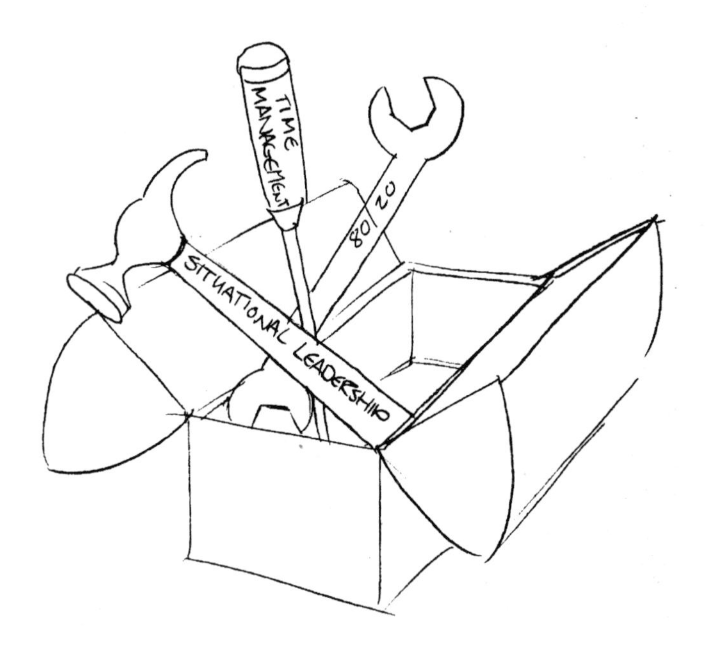

Any training, coaching, development activity or even a one to one conversation can benefit from your being able to draw on a number of 'tools' to use.

This is particularly so when it comes to dealing with your management population and, again, is a way of providing them with expertise in 'short bursts' as well as the everyday routine when it comes to giving them general advice.

When you are carrying out management training, for example, you will be 'tooling' people up, teaching the things they never knew before but that will now have the benefit of:

- Making them more effective managers
- Ultimately freeing up their time.

But this stuff doesn't just have to happen within a formal environment. You are carrying around your own 'toolbox' all the time and, inside or outside the training room, you can still deliver training to people in a quick but meaningful way.

There are hundreds of books on the market that deal with leadership and management; how to be a better manager, how to work better in a team etc. etc. You could choose any one of a thousand different tools but here are a few tried and tested ones to get you started that are, above all else:

- Practical
- Relevant
- Effective.

They may be about better people management or increasing the managers' own personal effectiveness but all can be delivered in around 15 minutes, over a coffee with a pad of paper to hand for those all important drawings and examples!

Time Management

'Quadrant 2' Management (From *First Thing's First* by Stephen Covey)[1]

Quadrant One	**Quadrant Two**
Deadlines Panic! Urgent Task	Planning Preparation Prevention
Quadrant Three	**Quadrant Four**
Other peoples' priorities Some meetings Some emails	Gossip! Junk Mail Trivia 'Popular activities'

The average working day or week can be divided into four quadrants in terms of activities.

The idea here is to try to spend as much time as possible in Quadrant 2 so that you don't have to spend as much time in Quadrant 1. Quadrant 2 time often comes from Quadrant 3.

---

[1] Covey, S (1994), Simon and Schuster UK, London

The week's calendar should be populated by Quadrant 2 activities first so that the individual is encouraged to carry out pro-active activities.

When people can apportion their activities into the four boxes, it soon shows how much time is being effectively wasted and that the real priorities are not being given the attention they deserve.

80/20 Thinking – Pareto's principle

As mentioned in **Lesson 4**, 80/20 thinking can really focus the mind on what is important and of most value.

Basically, it works around the principle that a small amount of input or effort can lead to the majority of outputs or results. Therefore a lot of your other effort or activities could be having little or no effect at all! In another way, 80% of the effects can come from 20% of the causes.

For example, in a department store 20% of the product lines may give 80% of the store's revenue. Working with the 20% of your managers with the worst employee turnover results may cure 80% of the issue. You have to therefore try to identify the right '20%' rather than trying to do everything.

It can be applied throughout the business and once individuals start to think 80/20 it can really help prioritise activities effectively and free up time to devote to the right things.

Situational Leadership (From *Leadership and the One Minute Manager* - KennethBlanchard[2])

A great tool to help managers spend the right amount of time with people rather than over - or under - managing them.

The main premise is built around the concepts of

- Competence
- Commitment

We will also revisit this in **Lesson 16** when it comes to managing performance. Situational Leadership asserts that people should be managed according to their level of competence and commitment with any given situation or aspect of their job role.

This is quite clever as it recognises that those who are competent and committed should be 'delegated' to, which in turn frees up your own time and allows others to flourish. Those with less competence or commitment specific to a particular task, for example, may require more 'direction' or 'coaching'. Whilst seemingly obvious, the tool is effective because managers can often end up re-treading old ground with people and constantly retraining or doing things for them. This can happen even when the errant individual is competent and can do things for themselves!

---

[2] Blanchard, K (2000) Harper Collins Business, London

The actions here are concerned with actually 'contracting' or agreeing with an individual their level of competence and commitment and then how they will be managed. If someone agrees they can be 'delegated' to then the accountability is theirs and the manager can focus their own efforts elsewhere.

Focus more on your best people

We spend too much time with our worst performers and not enough with our good ones. Managers will always get far more out of good people as opposed to the small amount of gain achieved from turning around underperformers.

The message is to deal with underperformance quickly and effectively (**Lesson 16**) and get back to your good people.

Managers should question what motivates their best people, what do they need, what are their aspirations, how much time have they spent with them this week?

Linked to this at the other end is …

Your Bottom 10%

There is always a core of underperformance in a business and there is usually always a 'bottom 10%' made up of the poorest performers.

Managers make the mistake of allowing this to fester and continue without being dealt with. Apathy can set in with a resigned 'that's just the way they are' approach. They can use the tools in **Lesson 16** to be continually dealing with the 'Bottom 10%' so that time is freed up for more productive priorities. Managers should always be asking: "Who is in this 10% and what am I doing about them?"

The Six Hat's[3] (From *Six Thinking Hats* - Edward de Bono)

People can develop limited ways of thinking. The six hats represent different approaches or 'hats' that people can 'wear' to look at things in different ways. Dealing with a problem, for example, may involve the 'putting on and taking off of many hats'.

Alternatively, it may be that everyone has to firstly wear a particular hat in addressing a current issue. For example, everyone needs to give their emotional responses first, thereby wearing the red hat. Later, the yellow hat will be worn and everyone then needs to look at the positives of the situation.

This helps people address issues and problems from a wide variety of angles. Those who only want to ever wear 'one hat' are therefore somewhat marginalised and are

---

[3] De Bono, E (1990) Penguin Books, London

more likely to have a stubborn, single minded way of approaching issues.

The Power of Three and Objective Setting

You learnt it in **Lesson 4** but a worthwhile use of 'The Power of Three' with others is when objective or goal setting.

1) Start with the main objective – make it **SMART** (**S**pecific, **M**easurable, **A**chievable, **R**ealistic and **T**ime-based)

2) Break it into three mini goals

3) Break each mini goal into three key activities.

This is a more effective way of focusing 80/20 style on what will have most impact. It also helps people take big objectives and systematically break them down to see how they can be more easily achieved.

For example:

Objective: Reduce smoking by two cigarettes a week so that I have stopped in six months time.

Three mini goals:

a) Improve my willpower

b) Follow a recognised programme to help stop smoking

c) Use a stop smoking aid

The three activities or 'how to' that accompany each mini goal:

a) i) Research ways to improve willpower

ii) Put methods into use

iii) Review progress weekly with activities

b) i) Research programmes such as those in the various 'Stop Smoking' self help books

ii) Carry out activities

iii) Review weekly progress

c) i) Internet research – which aids have best results?

ii) Try best one for you for a month

iii) Review results – alternatives?

If the individual didn't goal set in this way then they could go off on all sorts of stop, start tangents and it may take even longer to stop smoking!

There are obviously lots of tools you can use and lots of tips you will pick up over your career. This is just to give you a taster for the sorts of 'quick' things you can do with individuals as and when appropriate.

It's outside of the scope of this book but Neuro Linguistic Programming (NLP)is another technique that, once learned, can be coached to managers as a relatively quick and easy way to help people take a different approach at work and improve how they influence others.

Summary

- Build up a 'toolbox' of useful ways to help people improve their effectiveness as individuals or managers.
- These should be made up of relatively short exercises and pieces of teaching/coaching that are practical and relevant.

LESSON 16

MANAGING PERFORMANCE

It's only ever about the two columns and four boxes

'Now what?'

A business generally exists to achieve 'performance'. If it's a profit making enterprise then the people are ultimately contributing to it making more money.

This is fairly obvious and it's therefore logical that a lot of time is spent within businesses managing the performance of the people. When the words 'managing' and 'performance' are put together, however, they always seem to have a negative connotation. Phrases such as 'performance management' are bandied around and always have the element of doom attached to them.

Managing performance is also a pleasant experience though and can be about developing someone which has the effect of improving performance. It's also the case that high performers need other motivators to maintain or further improve their own performance.

HR has a clear role to play in the managing performance process. It is obviously involved in the training and development elements but the function is most widely used because of the legal framework attached to such activity when it is of the under performance kind!

As you have seen by now, however, I'm not interested in HR solely being brought in at the end to make something look 'good' legally when the line manager has laid down the law or done what they thought was right to move someone's performance forward. No, HR can again bring its expertise to the fore here, freeing the managers' time up and helping them to get it right first time, with no legal comeback.

This is where the true commercial approach of HR is put to the test as, often, someone else's underperformance can be the difference between the line manager failing or achieving their own targets. It is very high risk for them, very close to home and they want to achieve the right result – improve the individual or lose them!

Let's look at the determinants of performance to begin with.

Performance = Output

Own Activities using Skill, Knowledge and Attitude = Inputs

Other External / Internal Factors = Inputs

We will look more at skill, knowledge and attitude in the next lesson but, for now, let's put them into two columns:

Skill Knowledge	Attitude

We can then add to this with some other words that again do not cross over the middle line and remain in two distinct columns:

Skill Knowledge Competence Capability	Attitude Motivation Commitment Conduct

It may not at first sight be obvious but the left hand column focuses on whether someone 'can' do something and the right hand side generally focuses on whether or not they 'want' to.

Similarly, the words on the left hand side describe things that can generally be trained and on the right we have words that describe an individual's approach to something. It can be influenced but would be a stretch to say you could 'train' it.

There is another good reason for keeping these things separate in two columns: the legal framework. As you may know, two of the main grounds whereby you can legally dismiss an individual are for reasons of 'capability' or 'conduct'. By being clear what the reasons for underperformance are and understanding which column they fall into, so you can be clearer when it comes to any legal process then adopted in the future. This is where things get much neater and where, if involved with the line manager at the right time, you can ensure the process is logical and legal throughout.

To help with this, consider the four boxes below. They are a fantastic way of determining why someone may be underperforming and, in turn, what route of action should be taken. It even gives you a clear indicator as to whether you are in the realms of conduct or capability in legal terms.

Can/Does	Can/Won't
Can't/Tries	Can't/Won't

Can/Does – Often described as a 'can / do' person. No issues here!

Can/Won't – Has the capability, skill, etc. but, for some reason, attitude is poor and doesn't want to do it – Why? Look at attitude / motivation first.

Can't/Tries – Great attitude and commitment but just not 'getting it' – Needs training and support to increase capability.

Can't/Won't – Often don't last very long in businesses! – Disciplinary process usually kicks in very quickly if they haven't left the business already.

You can apply the four boxes to an individual as a whole or break it down into the elements of their role. For example:

Role: Secretary

Letters/Typing/Memo Activity – *Can/Won't*
Event Management – *Can /Does*
Presentation Preparation – *Can't/Tries*

The letters etc. activity requires a conversation focussing on why the individual won't do it and using potential disciplinary action as a last resort.

The presentation activity requires training to get them to a more competent level.

From a legal perspective the two most important boxes give clear routes:

Can/Won't – This often leads eventually to a disciplinary process to take corrective action so that the behaviour changes. Training is not normally required because the individual *can* usually do it.

Can't/Tries – After giving training and support it may be that formal action is required to highlight to the individual just how serious the situation is. Often, this is called a 'cautionary' or 'formal performance improvement' procedure as calling it 'discipline' implies it is corrective and that giving a 'disciplinary' warning to someone will magically make them better at their job!

HR's Role

So what is your role here? Well, it is to help the line manager work within the two columns and the four boxes above so that they choose the right actions to help improve performance.

There is no point in them focusing on training where it won't have an effect and there is no point in giving disciplinary warnings if the individual has never been shown how to do the job!

Your role is to help break down what is happening with the performance and question objectively so that you can help the manager go forwards. By partnering with the line manager on this you are both working towards performance improvement. The line manager is using your tools and expertise, e.g. the two columns and the four boxes to logically work through a situation that by now potentially feels quite frustrating, confusing and without any real progress.

Isn't this better than getting a call from a manager who has just reacted, done what they see fit and now the individual has walked out and is crying 'constructive dismissal'?

The conversation is relatively straightforward, here's an example:

David works in IT Helpdesk Support. Jenny is his manager and is concerned that he is not logging his calls, gives the wrong advice and is generally unhelpful and rude to those calling him with issues.

Jenny has phoned you, she has had enough and wants to give him a disciplinary warning.

This is a common type of situation. However, it is 'foggy'. There are multiple potential conduct and capability issues mixed in here.

You: "So, what reason would you give for the disciplinary?"

Jenny: "General poor performance."

You: "Oh!"

Managers use catch-alls like 'poor performance' in the absence of really analysing and breaking down an issue to then give clear actions and solutions.

If you then said 'OK fine' then a couple of things may be immediately apparent:

1) He appeals because he thinks the disciplinary is unfair. The manager hearing the appeal realises that he has been poorly trained and removes the warning, thereby affecting Jenny's credibility. David also now feels that he has the upper hand and it is now difficult to manage his attitude issues.

2) David accepts the warning but doesn't really know what he is doing, technically speaking. This hits his

confidence and he ends up resigning. Whilst Jenny is pleased, the next individual joining the team probably then suffers from the same lack of training as well!

So it doesn't always pay to go along with what the line manager initially wants to do as things need breaking down further:

David's performance:

Doesn't log calls **– Does he understand how to (Training?), Does he understand but can't be bothered (Attitude?), Does Jenny let other people off when they don't use the system? What's the custom and practice?**

Gives the wrong advice **– Has he given the right advice before (i.e. conduct issue, not capability), does he require training?**

Rude and unhelpful **– Has he always been? Why has his behaviour changed? Does this really need a disciplinary warning to address the situation?**

It is therefore beneficial to deal with the above as three distinct issues, even if there is a mix of disciplinary warnings and training then being administered. The point is that you and the manager are clear on what course of action is being taken to address which issue.

In my example, HR should then schedule review periods with Jenny to ensure she is delivering on her commitments, and in turn HR gets the opportunity with Jenny to evaluate David's progress.

This will enable Jenny to look at things differently the next time a situation arises. This kind of support is initially time consuming for HR but becomes less so as Jenny learns how to effectively manage others' performance.

Finally, as mentioned earlier, managing performance is also about maintaining and developing the performance of those 'can / do' people.

Your ideal is that you and your managers are not spending disproportionate amounts of time with your worst people. You will never get as much from them as you will from making your best even better.

So help your managers consider what motivates people to even greater success. This could involve:

- Them asking high performers to complete a motivation questionnaire
- Better use of incentives with them
- Involving them in projects and initiatives
- Getting them to mentor or buddy others
- Giving them a taste of managing others
- Asking their opinions.

...There are many ways to achieve this but it requires specific focus as often high performers are left to 'get on with it' and could become de-motivated and leave.

Summary

- Many things determine performance and can be broken down into two columns – a 'conduct' and a 'capability' column.
- The 'four boxes' point you to solutions in terms of how to manage performance.
- Use the 'two columns' and 'four boxes' to help managers separate issues and 'clear the fog' within performance situations.

LESSON 17

DEVELOP PEOPLE

but only to a point

This book has focused a lot around skill and knowledge because both of these words surround a great deal of the HR role, particularly for those who have a training and development remit as well. It is also one of those areas that can really make a difference to individuals, is often very satisfying for both parties and can have a great, positive impact on results.

Using the 'Power of Three' principles it is possible to adopt a framework like the one below to training and development:

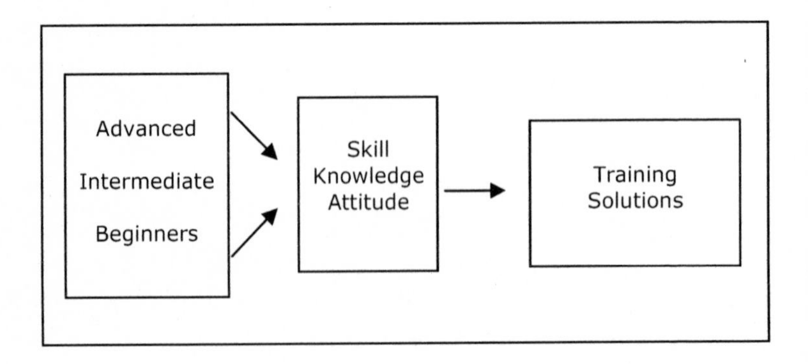

It is split into three levels: Beginners, Intermediate and Advanced which can refer to levels within a role or the three levels could represent different, successively more senior roles.

For each of these three levels it is then about focusing on the three elements of skill, knowledge and attitude required.

e.g. Customer Service Assistant – Intermediate

Skill: Resolve customer complaints first time.

Knowledge: Know company complaints procedure.

Attitude: Treat customers with respect, put themself in customers' shoes.

The next step is to come up with the training solutions that can help develop the skill and knowledge which in turn can also drive improvements in attitude.

This may involve a customer care workshop, ensuring there is a clear procedures manual or recommending books or self study modules that focus on customer service skills.

Importantly, in embarking on any training or development activity you first need to ascertain that the right attitude is present in the individual – or at least be clear that the training may then lead to the attitude the business is looking for. This is a bit like being back in school. If you have an unruly pupil who just isn't interested then there is no point in teaching them about the causes of the First World War. Inevitably, you end up repeating yourself or coming back to the subject again and again because the individual just hasn't *wanted* to learn it in the first place.

This is the same in business. Many trainers and managers will spend countless hours repeating the same training or development activity. Sometimes it has been genuinely forgotten or requires a refresher but more often the attitude just isn't there.

I have seen many trainers repeating training with individuals without really considering that they have 'been there before'. SOME of the information must have been learned and retained by the trainee, but it is normally the case that they have not put the training into effect back in the workplace and so require it again! This is a classic issue and the trainer needs to be able to say 'No' at some point and the focus switch to the attitude of the individual.

It is often useful to make reference to the Managing Performance square referred to in **Lesson 16**. My point above could be indicative of a 'can but won't' person.

Can/Does	Can/Won't
Can't/Tries	Can't/Won't

'Can't but tries' is your key box to rest on here.

If you can ascertain that the person *wants* the skill and knowledge, *has the right attitude* but just needs more training and support then this is what should be given.

But only to a point…

The 'Point'

The holy grail for a lot of training and development activity is to get great evaluation evidence that tells you the impact of your activities on the business. In a sales business, you can take a baseline of someone's performance, carry out some training activity and then look at the performance one month on, for example. You can then attribute elements of the training down to any success the individual then has. This is useful in knowing when to stop training someone, start training in a new area or repeat certain activities with them.

It does not follow that everything can be trained. For example, not everyone can receive management development coaching and then flourish as great managers. The clever bit is to know when to stop wasting valuable time when the output just isn't changing or developing positively.

E.g. you train a manager for the third time on ways to resolve conflict, how to weigh up options, be objective, look for win-win situations, reduce the causes of the conflict so it doesn't happen again, and so on…

One month on another difficult situation has cropped up and you have heard that the manager has yet again added fuel to the fire. Do you take him aside and retrain him again or is it pointless?

If you are sure that all other internal/external factors have been dealt with (e.g. the manager may have been overly provoked and so lost objectivity, are you indeed giving the right training – should someone else be involved?) then it is time to consider whether further training would be productive. This often leads to the word **Talent** cropping up.

Talent

'Next!'

The word 'Talent' is often defined as 'to possess natural aptitude or skill'. You could train someone to play football but it is their talent that determines how good they can be. Talent therefore is also about how well you can use or demonstrate a particular skill. This is important to know because many HR and training professionals obviously want to believe that they can improve anyone. This isn't always the case, however. In our example, the manager cannot resolve conflict and that may be because he may be naturally confrontational or lack diplomatic abilities. He doesn't have a 'talent' for resolving conflict. Therefore, he can be trained to a point but he may never really develop beyond that.

As we saw in the Managing Performance lesson, it is about knowing when enough is enough and when someone's lack of knowledge, skill or talent is having an unacceptable impact on the business. Often, HR can take an objective and more dispassionate view of this to bring clarity to a manager who is trying to determine the potential of one of their reports.

People are often described to be 'at level' and actually this is another way of saying that someone doesn't have the talent to go further. As another example, if a salesperson doesn't present well as a result of under confidence or because they have an awkward style then this could affect how well that person advances in their career. These may be innate weaknesses that are exposed because of the type of job the individual does.

This is not about giving up and admitting defeat though. In-house training and development may not be the answer, it may be that an external business coach or external training is required. Often, using external resources can give more confidence and confidentiality to the individual who is failing and not making progress through in-house support.

However, there needs to be enough skill or talent present in the first place to be able to nurture and develop it further.

The message is not to assume that everyone can be trained in everything but also not to give up on training and development too early. You need to assess:

- Is this a skill/knowledge issue that can be trained?
- Does their innate personality/behaviour/intellectual limitations etc. prevent them from ever being able to develop this skill?
- Have I considered all reasonable training and development interventions before abandoning further training or development?
- Have I stood back and watched the training being positively put into practice with the right results – have I seen the change in behaviour required?
- Has the person reached their 'level' within this skill/knowledge area?

It may be that you need to accept that this is a weakness that cannot be trained and move on to training the individual in another area or where they already have some strength.

The trainee's manager may be able to support the area that cannot be developed if the individual makes up for it with over performance in other areas. E.g. an individual may not be so good at dealing with underperformance in others so their manager may manage it with them when issues arise; more so than they would with other direct reports. Only when the weakness really interferes with the role (or the amount of support needed is onerous) should the manager consider using the managing performance aspects in **Lesson 16**.

Summary

- Align training and development activity to the skill, knowledge and attitude requirements.
- Consider the attitude of the individual before training skill and knowledge.
- Know when enough is enough – the individual may not be demonstrating the skill or using the knowledge effectively because they just don't have the talent.
- Talent can be nurtured but there has to be enough of something there to begin with!
- If you have gone as far as you can in one area, train them in something new where they have potential or develop an existing strength further.
- Consider with the individual's manager as to whether they can 'live with' and support the weakness.

LESSON 18
YOUR OWN BRAND
could you go it alone?

In recent years there has been an explosion in the number of HR people 'going it alone' as independent consultants or setting up their own small HR consultancy businesses. The attraction is obvious, particularly when it comes to servicing smaller businesses who cannot afford or justify employing their own HR people.

Some of these consultants are successful and some are not. Often, it can come down to factors such as financial awareness, sales skills, who you know and your functional skill level. However, what it also forces individuals to be is really clear of the strengths they can bring to businesses, how their approach is different and what really sets them apart from other consultants in the marketplace. When you are employed normally in a company you can become a bit complacent about these things because, barring any terrible underperformance on your part, you can safely say you have a job every day and managers generally have to 'buy' from you every day – they don't have a choice! Independent consultants rely entirely on the strength of their own brands to get them work, and brand management becomes an ongoing factor and a normal part of day-to-day life for them.

You may be thinking that it's a bit early on in your career to be thinking about going it alone. And you'd be right. But, to really challenge what you do in terms of adding value to your business and your overall style/approach, it is often a worthwhile exercise to 'think' like the independent consultant. This can really develop your credibility within your business as it encourages you to inwardly reflect daily on the questions:

Why do they employ me? What's my brand all about?

Let's break this down into a number of areas that have to form part of the independent consultant's mindset which you in turn can build into your own role.

Your Unique Selling Proposition (USP)

You may have heard of this before. This is about identifying the thing that makes you stand out from the competition. It may be in terms of a service or product offered in businesses or how your approach is different to others.

E.g. as an HR professional, you may have a particular dedicated specialism in something like Diversity or Employment Law, for example, that differentiates you from the other HR people in your business. Rather than being homogeneous, you can point to your specialism as something that few people have a skill in and where you are therefore of particular value.

You may have worked on the 'front line' before and so can profess to be more operational than other HR people. This could be unique in your business or not something they are used to having and so instantly can attract more 'points' than someone with a pure HR background.

So if you have a USP then develop this, communicate it regularly and ensure that the PR is out there so that people know that you are 'unique' in some way.

Describe it in 30 to 60 seconds!

'Your minute starts now'

As an independent consultant, one of the dreaded things I used to have to do was the 'one minute speech'. Basically, there would be a number of consultants present at a networking lunch.

Everyone then had one minute to stand up and explain what their business provided and why anyone should buy from you. This really is about stating the USP succinctly so that people are left interested and wanting to know more. Sometimes this is called the 'elevator speech' because you have to tell someone about yourself in the time it takes for a lift to reach its destination floor!

Critically, for an HR professional, it is about trying to convey how you are different from your peer group so that you are not just 'one of them'.

Again, particularly when you start out in the role, perfecting this type of elevator speech can really help when meeting new managers or stakeholders for the first time. They may ask:

'What do you do then?'

'How are you different from your predecessor?'

'What can you do for me?'

Enthusiastic, positive and professional

Those important behaviours that are of paramount importance. The HR professional is always looking positively to the solution rather than getting caught up in any doom or gloom! There is nothing worse than a manager telling you how difficult things are and you replying that you empathise and then tell them how difficult things are for you too! You are expected to stay positive and meet challenges head on with a 'glass half full' approach.

What are you like when it comes to the telephone? Do you return messages promptly, are you available when needed or do you have a reputation for never being there?

Do you do something when you say you are going to do it and always meet your deadlines? OK, some of these things can be quite difficult to do all of the time but they are the things that are going to make you memorable – you want people to say 'Why can't everyone be like her / him'?

When people feel positive towards you they will tell others (it works the same way when they feel negatively towards you as well – only they tell more people!). If others have a positive image of you then this will help develop their trust in you. If you make mistakes from time to time this is then often less of an issue for others, which can only be good for your stress levels!

Networking

The word strikes fear into some as a necessary evil! Others steadfastly refuse to do it as it is felt to be overly political or all about style and very little substance!

It really depends on why you would do it and your overall approach. If it is just to be seen and remembered then that's probably quite superficial. Networking should be about placing yourself in situations where you are meeting and interacting with new people where you can both be of use to each other. Alternatively, it may be about working more with senior stakeholders within your organisation that you would not normally be exposed to. This may be because you have asked to be involved in a new initiative or project that you are keen to work on, but it also gives you the added bonus of then being on the other person's 'radar'. This can help your influence within the business as well as potentially developing your career in the future.

Developing your relationships

There are some other simple, failsafe ways of developing your relationship with others:

- Admit when you have made a mistake
- Keep in regular contact and update people around your activities
- Have a contingency plan in case things go wrong
- Ask for feedback so you know how you are doing.

All of the above can apply equally to those in business on their own account and to those employed within businesses.

Thinking about your brand and how you might operate as an independent consultant is something you can do at any stage of your career. Starting out in a new role gives you a chance to review your brand and make any necessary changes or it may be that you have been in a role for a while and are newly reflecting on how you come across to others.

So, a final thought – you know why you might go to Marks and Spencer or use Virgin Atlantic, but do you know why people use you? Is it because they have to or because they want to?

Summary

- Approach your role as if you were an independent consultant where others are 'buying' from you because of who you are and what you deliver.
- What is your USP? Consider how you would distinguish yourself in terms of you as a 'brand'.
- Seek opportunities to network where it is of mutual benefit.
- Consider – do people deal with you because they want to or because they have to?

Lesson 19
The Future
managing your career

It is a sad and somewhat strange fact that HR people are often the last to upskill themselves. The problem is that they are so busy looking out for everyone else that they forget that this is a profession requiring its own ongoing development.

This reinforces any negative stereotypes around HR because the lack of upskilling means that there is less likelihood for personal development. This in turn can lead to the HR professional becoming so diluted in expertise that they become just another person in the business helping line managers and teams to get things done!

HR is developing all the time, with its latest fads and the spread of new ideas as in other professions. It is very easy to become out-of-date and then left behind when it comes to coaching, human capital management, employer branding and any other number of current concepts trying to help businesses achieve more, sometimes with less.

I don't want to just go through what is currently *en vogue* because it dates this book as things move on. However, you need to have a rolling plan of activities that are keeping you abreast of latest developments so you can assess their rightful place in your business as appropriate.

So let's go through a number of ways you can get ahead and stay ahead in the world of HR.

CIPD

As you will be aware, the Chartered Institute of Personnel and Development (CIPD) is the member body for the HR profession. They provide a wide variety of services to upskill their people:

- People Management – The CIPD magazine includes many articles and case studies around the latest developments in employee relations, reward, recruitment, training, development, effectiveness etc. as well as a case law employment law update for practitioners.
- Regional meetings – 'People Management' magazine also provides details of local group meetings, topics and guest speakers.
- Online services – Information, forums, reference points, updates.
- Library services for textbooks, journals etc.
- Training and development workshops and materials.

Take time to review CIPD's offering on a regular basis; get yourself on the online forums to find out how your peer group in other businesses are faring, how they are contributing to business success and the issues they face.

If you ever want to upgrade your membership you will need to provide evidence of Continuing Professional Development (CPD). There is a therefore an incentive here to ensure that you are always learning for yourself and your career. Progression through the CIPD levels is a great thing to have on your CV!

Management and leadership books

In **Lesson 15** we looked at the concept of the 'toolbox'. Many of these tools can be picked up from the latest and historically successful management and leadership texts. There are many famous business authors who have given practical, meaningful advice and direction over the years and it is a good idea to be as widely read as you can be.

This can often have a downside in that people then use a lot of buzzwords and business speak that do not really serve any useful purpose. However, used correctly, there are a number of practical tools and activities out there in these books that can really help people within business and make them more successful in terms of their achievements. It also works for you as well – such books can help you influence more effectively, approach problems and solutions in a more ordered way and help your clarity when it comes to strategy, priorities and appropriate activities.

HR texts

Again, there are a number of books that can help you not only on the specialist disciplines but also, as this book does, give you some guidance for how to approach and make a success of the generalist HR role.

Mentors

Find a mentor within your business who is not a stakeholder and can be objective and confidential and in whom you can trust. External business coaching is becoming more and more popular but having someone more skilled and experienced from within the business can be a real asset.

Other qualifications

Finally, consider other business qualifications that can improve your commercial awareness and business acumen. I have known people in HR study Masters Degrees and some even taking on MBAs. In time, this can develop your expertise and credibility immensely if you have the capacity to take on such a commitment whilst doing the 'day job'.

New projects, activities or initiatives

Get involved in something new that will really test you and take you out of your comfort zone. I believe that the best development for people is where they have been thrown into something at the deep end, are really challenged and have to learn new skills quickly. Often, this is accompanied by the churning stomach, even sleepless nights because it is something new and unfamiliar. This all sounds quite depressing but can often be the best way of really achieving sustained long term development.

There can only be one!

You're well into your role now and perhaps even on to your second or third HR role. At some point you will reach a crossroads. This may be in the form of the decision as to whether you should now work in a large corporate business, or whether you should move from a corporate to a much smaller company. It may be about deciding to specialise and take on an employee reward or internal recruitment role, for example.

You may want to consider whether you are better off continuing being part of an HR team or whether you would prefer to be in charge as the only HR generalist or specialist within the business (normally within smaller companies).

I would almost go so far as to say that a bunch of HR people together are often a bit of a nightmare! Many a time I have sat in large corporate businesses with ten HR people around a table. Often, it can be very frustrating as individuals come up with ideas and opinions on what they believe to be the right course of action for the business or a team, for example. This usually results in a kind of consensus around what HR *should* be doing. Often, however, one HR person's issues will not be somebody else's. What results is 'sheep dipping' where everyone has to run with the agreed activity or priority, whether it is relevant to them or not!

A lot of time can get lost in discussing things that may only really apply to a section of the business and this is where you have to then try and skilfully continue with your own priorities whilst mindful of the wider agenda.

A piece of advice I was given many years ago was to 'try and get yourself into a job where it is only you doing it'. Some of this makes sense and some of it doesn't. If you are the only HR Manager, for example, and you have a couple of direct reports then this is obviously going to make life slightly easier in terms of autonomy and the ability to make your own decisions. However, there is less of a support network around you and often people like the security of having colleagues to be able to call upon who understand the issues and can empathise.

Being the only one in a role does make you stand out more and in some ways, increases your chances of having a beneficial impact in the business because you can be more focused on your efforts rather than what other HR colleagues in other teams/units are doing.

There can be a greater sense of achievement where the buck stops only with you as opposed to being in a larger business and a 'cog in a big wheel'.

This works in the same way if you specialise; for example you may be the company's only employee relations professional. The learning curve is much steeper when you are the only one and, as always, real personal development only happens when you are put into difficult uncomfortable situations that you then learn and grow from.

Finally, look to the IT team within your business. Their world constantly changes as a result of technological advance. Most of them wouldn't dream of standing still and relying on knowledge and experience they had built up historically. They are reading around the subjects and keeping abreast of the latest thinking and what the future may look like. All of this can apply to the HR profession too; much of it may look like 'fads' but there will be some areas that really are the next big thing.

The identification of 'Generation Y' some years ago helped lead the thinking that working practices would need to change in the future, away from traditional structures and methods. This has now led to more flexibility in areas such as working patterns and the provision of employee benefits. The businesses that caught this trend early on will almost certainly have been able to attract and retain talent more effectively that those 'playing catch up'.

So, it pays to always be keeping one eye on future developments whilst managing the day-to-day activities.

Summary

- Don't fall into the trap of leaving yourself to last when it comes to your own learning and development.
- There are various solutions available to help you with this, particularly via the CIPD.
- Consider at some point whether you would benefit from being the only specialist within the business or carrying out a role that only you will be doing (HR Manager, for example).
- Being the 'only one' can often be more beneficial in terms of the satisfaction gained by achieving business objectives and working to an agenda that you have personally agreed with the business (distinct from potentially having to deliver someone else's HR agenda).
- Keep abreast of future developments around the 'world of work' so that you can build activities into your current plans that also address future challenges.

Lesson 20
A FEW FINAL TIPS AND TOOLS

Before we finish and look to the future, a few mini lessons for your 'toolkit' to help you along your way in HR.

The importance of 'matching'

This is a NLP (Neuro Linguistic Programming) technique and I pull this one out as it is an effective way of establishing rapport with the other person. Simply, this is about adopting the same body language, matching the tone or speed of their voice or other mannerisms. Obviously, you do not want to be doing everything the same at any given moment because that would look odd! It needs to be done in a very subtle, somewhat manipulative way to get on the same wavelength as the other individual.

If a manager is talking quickly and pacing up and down then you sitting still in a corner and talking quietly and methodically is probably not going to have much of an impact! You don't have to march up and down as well, but you do need to be aware of the need to perhaps be just a little more animated.

If someone is very colloquial and informal in their approach then be the same back to them. The points you are trying to get across can still be made but may now feel more receptive to the other person. This is often why so many of the best conversations seem to happen when alcohol is involved and people have their guard down. The talk is freer and, because everyone is now 'at the same level', people are generally more open, as opposed to being across desks in a more formal, office environment.

Beware of the domestic agenda

It is obvious that there will always be a certain amount of politics at play in business and different agendas will always be present, depending on key individuals' motivations. However, there is another context to this that I call the 'domestic agenda'.

If, as the HR professional, you are looking to be consistent and fair then often you will be focussing on what is right, rather than who is right or who has shouted the loudest! However, this is not always easy. There will always be the self-interest present in a situation where someone is looking to forward their own cause, sometimes at the expense of what has been applied before or simply what is logical. This, in some ways, represents the normal politics of business that I mention above. There is, alternatively, the concept of a person's argument driven by their own domestic circumstances.

An example:

Sarah wants to be promoted as she believes she is ready for the next level, with the job title, status and salary that accompanies it. This is despite her manager continually pointing out and attempting to address her performance gaps. Sarah believes that the company is being inconsistent, unfair and treating her differently from her peer group.

You could be tempted to spend a lot of time understanding how others have been promoted, why they are paid what they are and how decisions have been made in the past. This is all worthwhile and may still be appropriate but it is always worth understanding whether this is a company issue/mistake or an individual's personal issue/preference. Has Sarah got a case to argue –

is the company unfair or inconsistent or is she, instead, driven by her domestic need to earn more money? She may have financial difficulties, be the only person earning in the household or there may be a family expectation that she should have been promoted before now.

It is always important to ask the right questions and diagnose the *real issue* with people, rather than deal with the potential 'smoke and mirrors' created by the other person that can sometimes lead you down wrong paths.

Know the financial bits

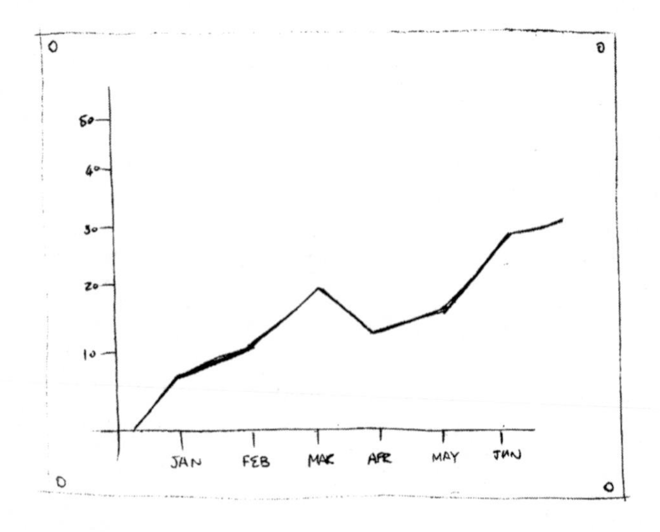

This book has concentrated on the need to achieve results for the business. Linked to this is the need to know the numbers, what's good and not so good and how your activities are affecting the figures.

E.g. a team may generate revenue of £1million but staff costs may be too high at £300,000 and rising.

Why is this? What has changed? Are employee turnover or absence rates increasing and putting pressure on the amount of overtime paid and temporary cover?

Perhaps people are working more inefficiently or the manager may have fewer skills when it comes to allocating resources. There are HR related issues here that can all be contributing to an eroding 'bottom line'.

The revenue, costs and profit lines are pretty straightforward to understand. However, it may be that you need to look deeper into conversion rates, how operating profit has been achieved, trends on a year on year basis, performance against budgeted targets. There are different ways of assessing the financial health of a team and the business.

If you are new to all this then do not just rely on people telling you their perception of the issues. Ensure you are included when it comes to financial reporting and read around the subject 'dummies' style to give you a good working knowledge.

Remember, HR is often seen as a cost centre, and most useful for controlling people costs. But through training and more effective recruitment, for example, HR can have a significant impact on the revenue line as well. Focusing on non-cost elements as well can therefore improve your commercial awareness and boost credibility as you are effectively influencing each of the main areas of the profit and loss account.

Organising yourself – The 'day book' and 'traffic lights'

Depending on whether you are in the same building or work remotely or geographically, you need to be able to organise yourself effectively. This is of the utmost importance in a HR generalist role as you will have many conversations with different people across a week and email may not always be the best way to keep track or hold a record of conversations and actions etc.

A day book is essentially a standard lined pad where you are recording critical conversations, action points, important information and other plans. It is much easier to be able to recall a conversation from months before if you are able to refer to a day book, diary style. You don't need every last thing in there but you need to develop a sixth sense about what may be important or need capturing in case you need to come back to it in the future.

Separately, a 20 or 40 pocket A4 folder is an effective way of separating current priorities, routines, projects etc. It is often separated into three parts:

- Red – Urgent and important activities, projects, priorities.
- Amber – Not as important or urgent but still needs to be regularly reviewed.
- Green – Normal routine priorities and activities that are not of great importance but may be the 'bedrock' small things that if ignored lead to bigger issues. (e.g. absence management statistics and associated activities may be in a Green section).

The 'Bedrock' – the everyday routines that happen before anything else

SO, what is this *bedrock* thing? Well, it's the activities that are part of the normal, everyday routine that everything else comes from.

For example, if people are paid correctly then this maintains motivation and productivity levels to a degree. If you stopped bothering to capture absence rates or do anything about them then things would soon suffer within the business. It's often about the routine administration, the 'hygiene factors' that someone has to do and it may well be your job to do them. It's all very well getting into the sexier bit of the job but the smaller stuff has to happen before anything else.

Often, as you develop in the role you will find better ways of doing the small things. Exit interviews may have become slicker or routine training may then be partly online in e-learning fashion, for example. But there is only so much that can be done in a less time consuming way. Even after years in a role the business still expects certain things to happen that you may have long ago perfected and become bored with!

There is always a basic Service Level Agreement (SLA) in place either overtly or implicitly. Your credibility will take a real knock if you are known for always wanting to get into the 'bigger, more strategic' stuff but can't be relied on to deliver the smaller, routine things.

Always be clear on the next six months

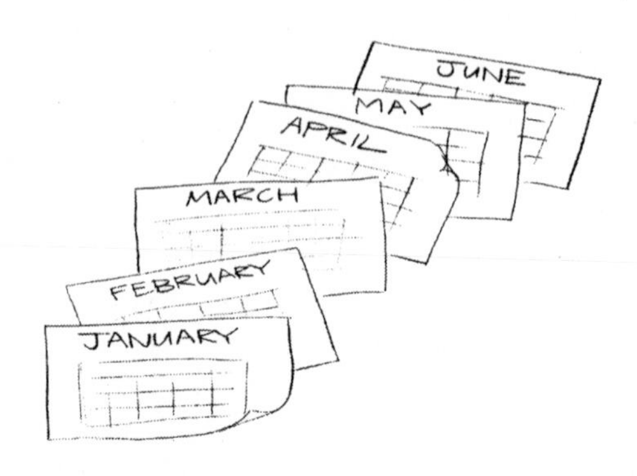

Many HR teams can get lost in planning ahead for years at a time. In the past I have been very involved in five year succession planning, for example, and this can be very difficult and sometimes useless depending on the nature of the business and other factors.

Always know as much as possible what the next six months is going to bring; there will be some knowns and some unknowns that you have to take a guess at. Working to a rolling six month plan encourages you to think ahead and to look at the business strategy and be considering HR activities against it both for now and what's required in the future. Encourage line managers to always be thinking six months ahead as well as it can often prevent having to deal with issues later on and at the last minute with the associated adverse effects this can sometimes have.

E.g. a manager has someone going off on maternity leave. What will be the impact on the team over the next six months and in six months' time? It is no good dealing with today's issues if her absence is going to lead to bigger issues in, say, four months' time when you know two other people are also leaving! The planning starts now to minimise future disruption to the business. Tomorrow always comes!

Six months in HR is a good timescale to be able to plan and organise effectively and to be able to draw different issues and priorities together and come up with the right activities.

The variables and unknowns after six months often skew things to the degree that you could be focusing on specific activities now to deal with things that may never happen in the future!

Summary – The Future – Beyond Beginner …

- As I said at the beginning, take from this book what you think will work for you and don't be afraid to make mistakes.
- HR is often illogical, frustrating and can sometimes feel without progress. However, balanced against this are all the successes you can have that make it such a varied and exciting role when you work hand in hand with the business.
- If you are hearing positives around how different you are compared to other HR people then that is often a good thing. People have an image of what they want HR in their business to be and often it can have the effect of pigeonholing people as cost centres and non value adding, particularly where there is a potential fear of HR!
- Deploy your expertise with credibility and get results – this removes any stereotypical perceptions and will expose you to areas of and activities within the business that you may otherwise have never got close to.
- This is what will give you the surefire key to developing an enjoyable, varied and successful career in HR.